Irish Histor 1700: A Guide to Sources in the Public Record Office

Alice Prochaska

Secretary & Librarian of the Institute of Historical Research

British Records Association

Archives and the User   **No. 6**

ISBN: 0 900222 077

TABLE OF CONTENTS

The cover picture, of the Fourt Courts, Dublin, is from *INF* 9.

FOREWORD

'Good wine needs no bush' and a quick glance at Dr Prochaska's work shows that it points to large, well-stocked cellars. Great Britain and Ireland have been linked throughout the ages by innumerable ties, political, economic, personal, and the multiplicity and variety of the relationships between the two islands is reflected in the contents of the Public Record Office, a remarkable number of its holdings having material of Irish interest. This material does not only reflect high policy – as mirrored in the Cabinet papers – and the evolution and working of the administrative machine, but also offers an immense amount of information about myriads of individual Irishmen, soldiers, civil servants, convicts, emigrants, policemen, testators, businessmen and bankrupts – providing raw material for scholars as far apart in interests and technique as the statistician and the genealogist. The value of the guide (and the pleasure of reading it) is greatly increased by its range which reveals how much of interest to the Irish historian is to be found in unexpected archival corners. As a result of the fusion of some Irish and British departments after the union, large deposits of Irish pre-union papers were transferred to London – fortunately perhaps in view of the great catastrophe of 1922 which rendered Wood's *Guide* to the contents of the Irish Public Record Office 'Alas unhappily only a guide to a cenotaph'. Consequently a considerable quantity of material relating to Irish trade and revenue in the 17th and 18th centuries is to be found in the papers of United Kingdom financial departments. More surprising perhaps is to come across information about Irish cattle in Isaac Newton's Mint papers, and in the records of the Department of Scientific and Industrial Research a report on Newry Town Hall. Sylvester Bonnard remarked 'that I do not know any reading more easy, more fascinating, more delightful' than a catalogue of manuscripts. He would have rejoiced at discovering Dr Prochaska's most helpful and stimulating volume.

R.B. McDowell

ACKNOWLEDGEMENTS

Numerous friends and former colleagues at the Public Record Office have taken a most helpful interest in this guide, and I am grateful to them all. The guide itself is based entirely upon the lists and other finding aids kept at the PRO, and so it is the work of many hands. I am also grateful to Ms Brenda Collins, of the Institute of Irish Studies, The Queen's University of Belfast, Professor R.B. McDowell, of the University of Dublin, Trinity College and Mr Trevor Parkhill of the Public Record Office of Northern Ireland, for some extremely helpful comments on drafts of the guide. Thanks are due, finally, to Dr Alan Thacker, the editor of this series, for his patient and meticulous editorial work. For the imperfections that remain, only I am responsible.

September 1985

Alice Prochaska
Institute of Historical Research
University of London

INTRODUCTION

The Public Record Office in London preserves and makes available the records of central government in England and Wales and subsequently the United Kingdom. It holds large quantities of material relevant to the study of Ireland from the middle ages onwards. Since so many of Ireland's own official records were destroyed in the disastrous fire at the Four Courts in Dublin in 1922, the documents in the Public Record Office in London constitute one of the largest collections within one institution of primary source material for the study of Ireland before 1900.* For Irish history since the partition of Ireland in 1921–2 and the creation of the Irish Free State, the intimate and tangled connections between north and south, and between Britain and both parts of Ireland, have ensured that the British public records continue to provide a rich source.

The contents of the Public Record Office are mainly, it must be emphasised, official records. They reflect the activities and interests of the British government in and relating to Ireland; the reason for their existence is almost always some official enterprise. But when that has been said, many readers may need to be reminded that at no time has government activity confined itself to 'important' citizens and institutions or to major political movements or questions involving only high policy. On the contrary, the intervention of government and its agents in the affairs of ordinary men and women has been continuous and complex, and is reflected over and over again in the public records. That is especially noticeable in the case of Ireland. In particular, it is by now a truism that 19th-century Ireland was an exception to the *laissez faire* doctrines which so often informed the policies of the governing classes on the mainland of the United Kingdom. It is even more true of official records relating to Ireland than to those of the United Kingdom as a whole that they contain an unmatched wealth of source material for the social and cultural history of the people, and of individual people.

While there is much to illustrate the darker side of Britain's relationship with Ireland (quantities of police files and other criminal records dealing with Fenianism, the constabulary, and law and order in general, for example), there is material also on all kinds of social, medical, cultural and other institutions. Customs records provide highly detailed information on Irish trade and industry, and also incidentally turn up such quirks as a volume of papers on Patrick O'Connor, an Irish gauger of shady reputation who was murdered in London in 1849. The 19th-century Treasury dealt directly not only with major institutions of government such as the Chief Secretary's Office and the Supreme Court, but also with the Irish National Gallery and Land Registry building have been so noted. All others, the great majority of those included in the guide, are kept at Kew and can only be seen there.

---

* At the time of the fire in 1922, official documents were being transferred from government departments to the Irish Public Record Office when they were about twenty years old. Work on the records of the Chief Secretary's Office had proceeded more slowly, with the result that only records up to 1789 had been transferred. Those from 1790 onwards survive and are kept in the State Paper Office in Dublin Castle.

the Royal Dublin Society. At the Magnetic Department, forerunner of the Meteorological Office, Sir Edward Sabine carried on a learned correspondence with Dr Humphrey Lloyd of Trinity College Dublin. Among the records of the Irish Sailors and Soldiers Land Fund in the 20th century are files dealing with the particular cases of ex-soldiers and ex-sailors, apportioned a new start in life in small-holdings and cottages all over rural Ireland. Such examples could be multiplied indefinitely. It is part of the intention of this guide to alert scholars to the rich diversity of sources on the Irish past contained in the Public Record Office in London.

This guide is not intended for the historian of Ireland before 1700. Irish records in Briitsh repositories (and especially in the PRO) have been rather more fully described already for the medieval and early modern period. For the abundant quantity of Irish material to be found in medieval and early modern records in the PRO, the reader should consult the *Guide to the Contents of the Public Record Office* and the printed lists, indexes, calendars, etc., to which that work refers. In the summary of PRO classes given below, the main reference codes of the earlier series of records are mentioned, partly in order to facilitate reference to the published *Guide* and partly because several of the series continue into the modern period. The present guide is designed to draw attention to the abundant sources for the history of modern Ireland which are in the United Kingdom Public Record Office and to identify the main reference headings under which they fall.

The records in the Public Record Office are grouped roughly according to their administrative provenance under letter codes such as *CAB* for Cabinet Office records, *FO* for Foreign Office records, and so on. These groups, and the many numbered classes within them, are described in alphanumeric order in the PRO's current *Guide*, part II, with their administrative context explained in the current *Guide*, part I, as well as in the published *Guide to the Contents of the Public Record Office*, cited above. These, as well as complete sets of detailed class lists, are available on the shelves of the reference room at Kew and in the search rooms at Chancery Lane. In this present guide the different sources of material for Irish history are decribed in alphabetical order of their PRO references, in the hope that this will prove to be the most useful arrangement for those who intend to consult the records themselves.

One of the difficulties the reader faces in using British public records as sources of Irish history, especially for the period after partition, is that of discovering to which part of Ireland particular records relate. File titles are all too often defective in this respect. Little attempt has been made here to clarify the position where descriptions in the PRO lists fail to do so: any such attempt would have prolonged unduly the time spent in preparing this guide. In many cases the reader will be able to infer the geographical basis from the context, but in others only the record itself will supply the facts. It is hoped that the brief outline of British administration in Ireland which follows this introduction will help the reader to assess whether records of a particular date or provenance are likely to meet his or her needs.

In the interests of brevity the compiler of this guide has relied mainly on the PRO finding aids described above. The records themselves, including manuscript registers and indexes, have been consulted only where the absence or presence of Irish material could not be established from the PRO's own description *and* there seemed good reason to suspect that there was Irish material to be found. The complexities of British and Irish administration have caused documents relating to Ireland to be created in any number of British government departments, and many public records not mentioned here no doubt contain valuable nuggets amongst material which at first sight might seem to be wholly void of Irish interest.

Where whole groups or large classes of records contain a distribution of Irish material throughout, they have been described only in general terms, leaving the individual researcher to seek more detailed guidance from the PRO's own guides and lists. Where there is a small amount of material in collections which otherwise appear barren of Irish relevance, it has often seemed necessary to provide more detailed description and examples. This unavoidably results in some imbalance in the amount of space given to particular records, with less useful classes often taking more than their share of description. The index rectifies this to some extent. It is prefaced by a list of all those classes which are devoted exclusively to Irish affairs.

Finally, this attempt to draw attention to the Irish riches among the British public records is intended only as a beginning. No exploration of such a diverse quantity of historical material can ever be complete.

Location and availability of records in the Public Record Office

The Public Record Office (PRO) is open to the public, free of charge, on three sites:

(i) *Chancery Lane, London WC2A 1LR* (telephone 01-405-0741)
Records of medieval and early modern government (to the late 18th century) and of the central courts of law in all periods. Reading rooms open 9.30 am – 5.00 pm on Monday to Friday except for public holidays and a two-week closure at the beginning of October.

PRO Museum. Open to the public free of charge. For current opening hours enquire at Chancery Lane.

(ii) *Land Registry building, Portugal Street, London WC2* (telephone 01-405-3488)
Reading room for microfilm of 19th-century census returns, which are available after 100 years.

(iii) *Ruskin Avenue, Kew, Richmond, Surrey TW9 4DU* (telephone 01-876-3444)
Records of 'modern' departments of state, mainly dating from the late 18th century but including some records of modern government departments and agencies which date back to the 17th century, and occasionally even earlier. It is at Kew that the great bulk of the records of modern government accumulate, becoming open to public view each year when they are a full thirty years old.
Reading rooms open 9.30 am – 5.00 pm on Monday to Friday except for public holidays and a two-week closure at the beginning of October.

In this guide those records which are to be seen at Chancery Lane or in the

Under the terms of the Public Records Act, 1967, a public record which has been selected for permanent preservation normally becomes available to the public at the beginning of the thirty-first year after the last date on the file, i.e. when it is fully thirty years old. In this guide, record classes which are still accruing or which only ceased to do so in the late 1950s or more recently are noted as covering the period from their starting date. New material may be expected to become available in these classes in the future under the 'thirty-year rule'. The final date of series which end in the early 1950s or before is noted.

There are a few exceptions to the 'thirty-year rule', and where these apply to the major part or the whole of a particular class they have been noted. It would not have been practicable, however, to note all the individual documents within classes which might be subject to exceptions, and occasionally particular items within open classes may not be available. The exceptions that can occur include: evidence given before royal commisions, which is often available immediately; records relating to security or intelligence matters, which are sometimes retained by their departments of origin or closed for periods ranging from fifty to one hundred years; records involving 'personal sensitivity', such as evidence in criminal cases, which may be closed for up to one hundred years; and records including information of a personal nature given in confidence by private citizens, of which the leading example is the census enumerators' books, kept closed for one hundred years. Readers who are in any doubt about the availability of particular material should consult the Search Department of the PRO at Kew in advance of their visit.

A brief outline of British administration in Ireland from the Act of Union

The complexities of Anglo-Irish administration have been described in a number of historical works, some of which are listed at the end of this section. Anyone conducting research in the public records who has not mastered their contents is likely sooner or later to be even more baffled than is necessary by the gaps and inconsistencies among the records. What follows here is a mere outline, designed to suggest in broad terms the connection between the records and their administrative origins. Short summaries of the administrative background are also given at the beginning of the entries for some particular groups.

The titular head of British adminstration and the representative of the Crown in Ireland until 1922 was the Lord Lieutenant or Viceroy. By the date of the Act of Union (which took effect from January 1801) the Chief Secretary had become more prominent in Irish administration, although the holders of both offices were usually members of either the House of Lords or the House of Commons at Westminster, and throughout the 19th century one or other of them was usually a cabinet minister. While the Chief Secretary travelled between London and Dublin, his principal scene of operations and administrative apparatus was in Dublin, with an Irish Office in London acting mainly as a channel of communications between the Dublin administration and all those departments of the British government which became involved in Irish affairs.

Some British government departments became so deeply involved in Irish administration at different levels that they established their own direct communications with Dublin early in the 19th century, more or less bypassing the Irish Office in London, though they usually still worked through the Chief Secretary's Office in Dublin. The most important were the Treasury and the Home Office. The Irish Treasury was fused with the British Treasury in 1816 under the terms of the Act of Union, and by the 1830s all Irish revenue collecting and the auditing of Irish accounts were firmly supervised from London. British Treasury ministers from then on therefore shared with the Chief Secretary the responsibility to Parliament for Irish affairs. Other Irish financial institutions which by then had been dissolved and their functions transferred to their British equivalents included the Quit Rent Office and Forfeiture Office and the Commissioners of Stamps, all of them broadly subject to Treasury oversight. Separate Irish departments which came directly under the control of the British Treasury included the Board of Works, the Valuation Office and (from its foundation in 1879) the National School Teacher's Superannuation Office. The official representatives of the British Treasury in Ireland were the First Lord of the Treasury for Ireland and the Paymaster of Civil Services, but after 1861 British Treasury ministers took over their responsibilities directly. The period of the Great Famine in the 1840s had already brought the Treasury into even closer contact than before with Irish administration when Charles Trevelyan (then assistant secretary to the Treasury charged with Irish relief), working mainly in London, used the head of the Irish branch of the Commissariat and the chairman of the Irish Board of Works and his principal agents in Ireland for the operation of relief. The subject indexes to Treasury in-letters between 1830 and 1920 (*T108*) and other records reveal vast quantities of Irish correspondence at all periods and at all levels. Even after partition and the independence granted to the Irish Free State in 1922, the British Treasury continued to deal not only directly with the government of Northern Ireland but also with a large residue of business arising in one way or another from its former functions in the whole of Ireland.

The Home Office had general oversight of all civil and some military administration in Ireland through the Chief Secretary's Office and the Irish Office. It also kept a residual jurisdiction which it exercised in times of emergency, for instance by taking over direct control in 1916 during the temporary vacancy of the chief secretaryship. Among the various duties which came directly under the Home Secretary in normal times was the responsibility for grants, commissions and appointments. A close supervision of civil order and policing led to the appointment of a special assistant on Irish affairs within the Home Office at the time of the Fenian disturbances in 1867. In 1922 the Irish Office became the Irish Branch, directly responsible to the Home Secretary for the affairs of Northern Ireland. Two years later the branch was dissolved and the Northern Ireland Department (G Division) of the Home Office was formed. The Home Secretary assumed direct responsibility in 1924 for relations with the government of Northern Ireland, for safeguarding the constitution of the province and for naturalisation, control of aliens and extradition; until 1926 he also exercised in Northern Ireland some powers assigned to the abortive Council of Ireland. The Home Office also took over from the Colonial Office in 1923 questions relating to pensions of the disbanded Royal Irish Constabulary, their administration and payment remaining the concern of the Paymaster General. The *HO* group of records therefore reflects a very wide range of business concerning Ireland.

A third major department of the British government, the Colonial Office, had relatively little to do with Irish administration before 1922, but inherited at that date both responsibilities and records. From 1922 until the formation of the Dominions Office in 1925, it dealt with relations with the Irish Free State. The renamed Irish Branch (formerly Irish Office), which reported to the Home Secretary in respect of Northern Ireland, did so to the Secretary of State for the Colonies in respect of its dealings with the government of the Irish Free State. After its abolition in 1924, reponsibility for relations with the Irish Free State passed to the Dominions Office. In the years 1922 to 1925 the British Colonial Office had handled relations between the two countries at a time of enormous change and activity. It had also inherited the records of the old Irish Office, while those of the Chief Secretary's Office in Dublin were kept by the government of the newly-formed state and, mercifully, escaped for the most part the fire in the Four Courts in 1922. The continuation of functions reflected in *CO* records for the period 1922–5 is to be found in those of the Dominions, later Commonwealth Relations, Office in the *DO* group.

Several other departments of the British government dealt with Ireland continuously and in important ways. The Cabinet, and later also the Prime Minister's Office, held and continue to hold responsibility for the central direction of policy towards both parts of Ireland. Although Cabinet records for the period prior to the major changes in Cabinet organisation of 1916–17 are relatively sparse, they contain even among the earlier classes a high proportion of papers relating to Ireland. Central direction of policy was also, in another sense, the responsibility of the military departments: the Ordnance Office, Board of Ordnance and War Office, the Admiralty and Navy Board and, in the 20th century and to a smaller extent, the Air Ministry and Ministry of Defence. Before 1801 the Lord Lieutenant, and through him the Chief Secretary, were responsible in general for the defence and military establishments of Ireland, but after the Act of Union all powers of appointment to regular army regiments and military command passed to the Commander-in-Chief in England. Until their abolition in 1855, the Ordnance Office and Board of Ordnance were responsible for such matters as barracks and military supplies, and this in practice involved them very considerably in Irish affairs. After 1855 these functions passed to the War Office. Also permeating Irish life at every level from an early date were the officials of the Board of Customs, Board of Excise and Board of Customs and Excise, and the Board of Stamps and of Inland Revenue, leaving among their records rich sources of information on Irish economic and social history. Legal administration, prisons and most local questions of law and order came for the most part directly under the Chief Secretary in Ireland, and a very different system from the British developed there. Yet even in the case of the law, British courts and legal departments of government inevitably became involved, and an Irish law officer usually sat in the British Parliament. The Lord Chancellor's Office was only one example of a department with juridical powers involving Ireland, and the court of Chancery only one of the courts in which cases involving Irish lands and individuals might be heard. Nor, of course, were Irish offenders in England exempt from the jurisdiction of English courts.

When all the links between British and Irish administration have beeen explored, it remains true that most Irish history, both administrative history and the broader history that flows from administrative origins, must be sought in Ireland itself. The chief source is in the surviving records of those organisations which were set up independently of, though sometimes in parallel with, the administrative institutions of Great Britain. The National Board of Education (established in 1831), the Irish Local Government Board (1872), the Land Commission (1881), Congested Districts Board (1891) and Department of Agriculture and Technical Instruction (1899) are only some of the best known and most important departments whose administration remained altogether separate from departments with similar functions for England, Scotland and Wales. Even these, however, perforce had dealings with the British Treasury and left abundant traces of their work among Treasury records.

The establishment of the Irish Free State in 1922 brought to an end the old administrative structure, the offices of Lord Lieutenant and Chief Secretary, and the apparatus of financial control. What replaced it in the Irish Free State was a new and independent governmental structure, dealing directly with the British government, at first though the Irish Branch and Colonial Office, then through the Dominions, subsequently Commonwealth Relations, Office. In Northern Ireland, with its separate parliament and devolved government, the relationship was much more intricate, though the main channels for dealings between the two parts of the United Kingdom were the Treasury and the Home Office (replaced in this capacity only in 1972 by the newly-created Northern Ireland Office). The British Cabinet and Prime Minister's Office, and to some extent the military and defence departments, retained an obvious, continuing interest in relations with both Northern Ireland and the Irish Free State (soon afterwards to become known as Eire). So too did the Treasury and other British financial departments, both in the continuing responsibility to provide some financial administration in Northern Ireland and in the residuum of centuries of financial responsibility in Ireland as a whole. The summary of classes of records which follows here reveals further links between Great Britain and Ireland, both north and south, in numerous administrative areas, some of them rather unexpected.

Records of the Chief Secretary's Office and other records of British administration in Ireland, together with those of the subsequent relations between Great Britain and Eire, are in the State Paper Office, Dublin Castle, and the Public Record Office of Ireland, Four Courts, Dublin 7. Records of British adminstration in Northern Ireland are held (and continue to accrue) at the Public Record Office of Northern Ireland, 66 Balmoral Avenue, Belfast BT9 6NY.

SELECT BIBLIOGRAPHY

The following works (among many others) will be found most useful:

J. C. Beckett, *The Making of Modern Ireland, 1603–1923* (London, 1966)

P. Bew and H. Patterson, *The State in Northern Ireland* (Manchester, 1981)

P. J. Buckland, *The Factory of Grievances: Devolved Government in Northern Ireland* (Dublin, 1979)

R. J. Hayes, editor, *Guide to the Sources for Irish Civilisation* (11 vols., Boston, Massachusetts, 1965); *First Supplement, 1965–75* (3 vols., Boston Massachusetts, 1979)

M. Laffan, *The Partition of Ireland, 1911–25* (Dublin, 1983)

R.J. Lawrence, *The Government of Northern Ireland: Public Finance and Public Services, 1921–64* (Oxford, 1965)

F. S. L. Lyons, *Ireland since the Famine, 1859 to the Present* (London, 1971)

R. B. McDowell, *The Irish Administration, 1801–1914* (London, 1964)

T. W. Moody, F. X. Martin and F. J. Byrne, editors, *A New History of Ireland*, vol. viii: *A Chronology of Irish History to 1976* (Oxford, 1982)

J. A. Murphy, *Ireland in the Twentieth Century* (Dublin, 1975)

The following journals contain much material of interest:

Irish Historical Studies: the joint journal of the Irish Historical Society and the Ulster Society for Irish Historical Studies (Dublin, from 1938)

Irish Archive Bulletin: the journal of the Irish Society for Archives (Dublin, from 1971)

Irish Economic and Social History (Dublin and Coleraine, from 1974)

Saothar: the journal of the Irish Labour History Society (Dublin, from 1976)

The following PRO Guides are indispensable:

Guide to the Contents of the Public Record Office (3 vols., London, HMSO, 1963–8)

Current *Guide* to the contents of the Public Record Office. This *Guide* is updated at frequent intervals. Part I, which contains administrative histories of the government departments, is available at present only at the PRO; parts II and III, class descriptions and index, are available on microfiche and may be purchased from the Photo-Orders Section of the PRO, Ruskin Avenue, Kew, Richmond, Surrey TW9 4DU.

SUMMARY OF CLASSES OF PUBLIC RECORDS WHICH CONTAIN MATERIAL OF RELEVANCE TO IRISH HISTORY FROM 1700

Listed in alphabetical order of Public Record Office reference codes.

ACT: Government Actuary's Department

The Government Actuary's Department, formally established in 1919, inherited duties under the National Insurance Act, 1911, but was also widely consulted by government departments on questions not concerned with national health insurance. For example, it carried out work on unemployment insurance on behalf of both the UK Ministry of Labour and the Northern Ireland Ministry of Labour. Under the National Insurance Act, 1946, it became one of the government actuary's additional duties annually to review the working of the whole national insurance system and to conduct a comprehensive financial inquiry every five years in Great Britain and Northern Ireland. A multitude of other actuarial and advisory duties bring the department into contact with the numerous institutions of both local and national government. For related records dealing with insurance and national health see *MH* and *PIN*. There are only two classes of *ACT* records:

ACT 1 Correspondences and Papers, from 1870. References to Ireland are scattered throughout this class. They include, for example, papers on National Health Insurance in the Irish Free State, 1922–3, widows', orphans' and old age pensions schemes for Northern Ireland and the Irish Free state, 1925–33, a quantity of files on unemployment insurance in Northern Ireland, and advice to the Northern Ireland Ministry of Labour on the Beveridge plan.

ACT 2 Approved Societies: Representative Papers on Valuations, 1918–1948. This small class contains the valuations of a representative sample of approved societies, some of which (e.g. the Catholic Benefit and Thrift Society) may well have had a proportion of Irish Members.

ADM: Records of the Admiralty and related departments

Irish material will be found scattered throughout *ADM* records. Admiralty and naval personnel, for example, are recorded in many different ways in service and pensions records as well as in the logs, war diaries and other records of ships and stations in which they served. A PRO leaflet, available free of charge, provides an introduction to Admiralty records as sources for biography and genealogy. Records relating to British coastal defence and to naval operations in the seas surrounding Ireland also, of course, contain abundant references to Ireland. In many cases these can only be traced, laboriously, by the historian who already knows exactly what he or she is looking for. The following classes should be noted in particular:

ADM 1 Admiralty and Secretariat Papers, from 1660. This is the main series, at first of in-letters, later of files relating to the whole range of Admiralty business. Irish affairs therefore occur in many parts of the class. Papers from 1938 are listed under subject codes, with matters relating to Ireland under code 33. Indexes and digests are in *ADM 12*. From 1852 case papers, i.e. large collections of papers relating to particular cases, including affairs of Ireland and the Irish Republic, were kept separately and are to be found in *ADM 116*. Case papers of the First and Second World Wars will also be found in *ADM 137* and *ADM 199* respectively.

ADM 2 Admiralty and Secretariat Out-Letters, 1656–1859. They are listed under subject headings (e.g. orders and instructions, secretary's letters, letters relating to convoys, to courts martial, to marines, to ports, yards and stations, secret orders and letters, etc.), many of which include a scattering of references to Ireland.

ADM 7 Admiralty and Secretariat Miscellanea, 1563–1932. The class includes coastguard reports relating to Ireland in the 1830s and 1840s and reports by the Irish officers F.L. McClintock and F. Mecham from Arctic expeditions of 1850–4. Other material of Irish interest may well be found in this class.

ADM 12 Admiralty and Secretariat Indexes and Compilations, Series III, 1660–1938. They include the Admiralty digest (subject indexes) and indexes (which are to persons and ships) and refer to *ADM 1, 3* (Admiralty Board minutes) and *116*. The class also includes a digest relating mainly to papers in *ADM 2* between 1763 and 1792.

ADM 49 Accounting Departments, Various Papers, 1658–1862. These miscellaneous papers include one bundle (*ADM 49/111*) relating to Irish signal stations, 1804–7.

ADM 106 Navy Board Records, 1659–1837. This large and miscellaneous class includes in and out letters, entry books, indexes and digests (for the distinction between indexes and digests in *ADM* records, see *ADM 12*, above) minutes, registers and a range of other miscellaneous papers. There is much relating to stores, supplies and contracts for the navy and naval dockyards which in the 18th and early 19th centuries involved much traffic with Ireland.

ADM 116 Admiralty and Secretariat Cases, from 1852. Large collections of papers relating to particular cases. Before 1852 they were kept with the other records which are not to be found in *ADM 1*, and case papers for the two World Wars will also be found in *ADM 137* and *199* respectively. *ADM 12* (see above) contains some indexes and digests to papers in this class.

ADM 137 Historical Section, 1914–18 War Histories, 1900–24. A collection of material for the Admiralty's official history of the First World War, arranged chronologically and by areas of operations. To some extent it overlaps in subject-matter with records in *ADM 1* and *116*.

ADM 148–50 Ireland Station Records, including indexes, 1816–1912.

ADM 199 War History Cases and Papers, 1938–49. Case papers dealing with naval administration and naval operations of all kinds during the Second World War. Similar papers for the First World War are in *ADM 137* and for other periods in *ADM 1* and *116.*

ADM 178 Admiralty and Secretariat Papers and Cases, Supplementary Series, from 1892. Sensitive items were extracted from *ADM 1, 116* and *167* (Boards of Admiralty minutes) and put into this class, most of which can only be seen by readers who have signed a declaration to respect the confidentiality of the papers. They include papers on naval matters affecting the Irish Free State, some of which may be seen without the restriction that applies to most of the class.

AIR: Records of the Air Ministry and related departments
Operations of the Royal Air Force in Ireland and over the Irish Sea are reflected in several classes of *AIR* records, and many can be traced with the aid of the subject index kept by the Air Historical Branch, a copy of which is on the reference room shelves at the PRO, Kew. In addition to the Air Historical Branch records (*AIR 1* and *5*), the operations records books of RAF commands, groups, wings, etc. contain records of operations in Ireland, and classes of more general correspondence will also be well worth searching. The likeliest sources are mentioned below.

AIR 1 Air Historical Branch Records, Series I, from 1862. Most of the papers in the class relate to the First World War and were removed from among the registered files of the Air Ministry (*AIR 2*) for use in official histories of the ministry and of particular squadrons and operations. They also include files which originated in the Admiralty, Ministry of Munitions and War Office. The series is continued in *AIR 5*.

AIR 2 Correspondence, from 1887. Files of registered correspondence of the Air Ministry, including files of the two Air Boards which preceded it and of the Admiralty and War Office. Those collected for the purposes of the official histories and covering dates up to 1930 are *AIR 1* and *5*.

AIR 5 Air Historical Branch Records, Series II, from 1914. They continue series I (*AIR 1*) and consist mainly of files opened between 1921 and 1930.

AIR 8 Records of the Chief of the Air Staff, 1914–47. The class includes papers on Dominion and other air forces and on the release of aircraft to Eire during the Second World War, and several pieces on operations in Ireland in 1920–2, with minutes of the Cabinet Committee of Imperial Defence (C.I.D.) sub-committee on Ireland, 1920–2.

AIR 9 Records of the Director of Plans, 1914–47. Piece 48 deals specifically with the Irish Free State, 1925–35.

AIR 24–9 Operations Records Books of Commands, Groups, Wings, Squadrons, Stations and Miscellaneous Units, from 1911. The daily record of events in each command, etc., supplemented with documentary appendices. Stations, etc. in Ireland appear with the rest.

AIR 50 War of 1939–45 Combat Reports, 1939–45. Combat reports of various squadrons, wings and groups, including those of some Commonwealth and Allied units based in the UK, and of some individual officers.

AO: *Records of the Audit Office and Exchequer and Audit Department*
The Exchequer and Audit Department exercises the functions of checking and auditing public accounts under the terms of the Exchequer and Audit Departments Act, 1867. Its functions date back to the reign of Henry VIII, and from time to time it has absorbed other departments, including in the 1830s the Irish Audit Office. Its complex administrative history is described in the PRO's current *Guide*, part I (section 202). Records of the Irish Audit Office itself appear to have ended up in the Irish Public Record Office, but there is a considerable amount of Irish material among *AO* records. The great range of Irish institutions of every size and degree of importance with which the Exchequer and Audit Office dealt makes its records a rich collection of source material not only for the administrative and financial but also for the broader social, economic and cultural history of Ireland, particularly in the 19th century.

AO 1 Declared Accounts (In Rolls), 1536–1828. Material dealing with Irish finances is usually to be found on rolls dealing with other business, but occasionally on rolls devoted exclusively to Irish business. See especially *AO 1/284–91*.

AO 2 Declared and Passed Accounts (In Books), 1803–43. Irish accounts are scattered throughout the class. Continued in *AO 20*.

AO 3 Various Accounts, 1539–1886. Include Irish accounts, 1837–67. See also *AO 19*

AO 11 Establishments and Registers, 1604–1867. Include registers of the civil and military establishment in Ireland, 1604–29.

AO 17 Records of Absorbed Departments, 1580–1867. The class includes various Irish accounts, in particular the records of the Commissioners of Imprest Accounts in Ireland and of the commissioners for auditing the accounts of Ireland, 1776–1833.

AO 19 Current Accounts, 1801–1906. These accounts, which were declared before the Chancellor of the Exchequer, are the more detailed versions of the declared accounts of which abstracts appear in *AO 3*. A large proportion relates to a wide variety of places and institutions in Ireland, ranging for example from hospitals and lunatic asylums to local constabulary.

AO 20 Accounts Declared before the Chancellor of the Exchequer, 1849–66. A continuation of *AO 2*, the class list includes a subject index showing a quantity of Irish subject matter. This is indexed both under particular subjects under Ireland and under Dublin: Chief Secretary's Office.

AP: Records of the Irish Sailors and Soldiers Land Trust, 1923–64

The trust, constituted under the Irish Free State (Consequential Provisions) Act, 1922, first met in 1924 to provide cottages, with or without land, in Ireland for men who had served in the armed forces during the First World War. It had headquarters in London and offices in Dublin. Much of its business is also reflected in *HO 45* (see below). The *AP* group as a whole is a rich source for the history of housing and social conditions, local government and institutional rivalries in Ireland from the 1920s until the end of the Second World War.

AP 1 Correspondence Files: Southern Ireland, from 1924.

AP 2 Correspondence Files: Northern Ireland, from 1924.

AP 3 Correspondence Files: Headquarters, from 1923.

AP 4 Minutes, from 1924.

AP 5 Register of Properties in Northern Ireland, 1923–7.

AP 6 Accounts Ledgers, from 1924.

ASSI: Records of the Clerks of Assize

(NOTE: Kept at the PRO, Chancery Lane)

These are the records of judicial proceedings in the Assize courts on the various circuits of England and Wales. They do not relate to judicial proceedings in Scotland or Ireland, but will include records of the trials of Irish people at assizes in England and Wales. They are potentially useful, therefore, for biographical and genealogical purposes, in which respect they supplement the criminal papers in the *HO* group described below. The records include minute books, indictments, depositions, pleadings and miscellaneous returns, and are arranged according to the circuits covered by the Assize judges. They are descibed in the published *Guide to the Contents of the Public Record Office*, vol. I.

AST: Records of the various Assistance Boards which have been responsible for the administration of social welfare

The administration of unemployment assistance, old age pensions and other forms of public assistance was carried on before 1934 by a number of different departments including the Customs and Excise, Board of Trade, Ministry of Health and Ministry of Labour. In 1934 the central administration of unemployment insurance was transferred to an Unemployment

Assistance Board. In 1940 this was reconstituted as the Assistance Board and took over responsibility for supplementary old age pensions, with subsequent accruals of responsibility for other forms of pensions, maintenance payments and the general relief of distress during the 1940s. This board in turn became the National Assistance Board in 1948. *AST* records include some inherited from other departments relating to their administration of public assistance in its several forms. Material relating to administration in Northern Ireland and to problems affecting Irish people in England and Wales will be found scattered throughout *AST* classes. Some examples are given below.

AST 7 General Files, 1910–65. They cover an extremely wide variety of welfare work and are arranged under file titles with a subject index at the front of the class list. Among scattered references to Northern Ireland are *AST 7/603*, allowances in Northern Ireland, refunds of excess payments, 1942–3; and *AST 7/508* and *820*, supplementary pensions, reciprocal arrangements with Northern Ireland, 1940–5 and 1946–7.

AST 15 Non-Contributory Old Age Pensions, Customs and Excise Files, 1908–47. *AST 15/9* is a file dated 1908–10 on the method of estimating the income of old age pension claimants in occupation of land or maintained on farms in Ireland.

AVIA: *Records of the Ministry of Aviation, Ministry of Supply and some others*

AVIA 22 Registered Files of the Ministry of Supply, from 1934. This very extensive class relates mainly to the war-time functions of the ministry, which was created in 1939 to deal with the supply of munitions and other military needs. The ministry came to be involved in coordinating supply and demand, including that for raw materials and labour in all essential industry, in the principal basic trades, and scientific research. Material of relevance to Ireland will certainly be found in many files dealing generally with aspects of the ministry's work. The following are some examples of files specifically listed as relating to Ireland: *AVIA 22/745*, publicity for a salvage campaign in Northern Ireland, 1940–1; *AVIA 22/1184–92, 1332, 1338*, files on the recruitment of labour and utilisation of resources in both Eire and Northern Ireland, 1941–5; *AVIA 22/3067–8*, sources of supply of iron ore in Ireland, 1940–3; and *AVIA 22/3297–8*, use of manufacturing capacity in Eire and imports of raw materials from Eire, 1939–40.

B: *Records of the Courts of Bankruptcy and Court for the Relief of Insolvent Debtors, and associated records*
(NOTE: Kept at the PRO, Chancery Lane)
Bankruptcy and associated records include those of cases relating to Irish bankrupts in England. Among other things they are a rich source for business historians, and will be found to include information on enterprise in Ireland

as well as on Irish businesses and individuals in England, Scotland and Wales. They are arranged in the following classes:

B 1 Order Books, 1710–1877. The class includes order books of the Court of Review. Each volume is indexed. Pieces 213–14 are registers of orders in the Court of Review, 1832–77.

B 2 Court of Bankruptcy Miscellanea, 1831–69. The class includes lists and registers of attorneys and solicitors admitted to the Court of Bankruptcy and gaolers' returns from Queens, Whitecross Street and Horsemonger Lane Prisons, 1862–9.

B 3 Commissions Files, 1759–1911. Many of these are indexed in *B 4*, docket books, or registers of commissions, 1710–1849. They are listed by date and name, and are open to inspection only when they are 100 years old.

B 5 Bankruptcy Court Enrolment Books, 1710–1855. Arranged in a general series and then under certificates of conformity and assignments, with one volume of examinations, depositions, etc. and three volumes of fiats, 1832–55.

B 6 Registers of the Commissioners of Bankrupts, Court of Bankruptcy, Court for the Relief of Insolvent Debtors, High Court of Justice in Bankruptcy and London Bankruptcy Court, 1733–1886.

B 7 Minute Books of Proceedings in Bankruptcy Appeals, 1714–1875.

B 8 Indexes to Bankruptcy Enrolment Books, 1820–70.

B 9 Proceedings under the Bankruptcy Acts, 1832–1902. A selection retained because they were considered to have some permanent public interest. They are listed by date and name with the occupation given beside each name. Open to inspection when they are 100 years old.

B 10 Proceedings under the Joint Stock Company Acts, 1856 and 1857, 1858–60. Selected on the same criteria as *B 9* above.

B 11 Registers of Petitions, 1884–1911.

B 12 Registers of Receiving Orders, 1887–1912.

BJ: Records of the Meteorological Office and its predecessors
The records transferred to the Public Record Office from the Meteorological Office since about 1975 include both administrative papers and the personal working papers of some eminent 19th-century scientists. References to Ireland do not abound, but the class lists are worth searching nevertheless for correspondence with individual Irish scientists, meteorological observations connected with Ireland, and other material. The following references are the only ones of obvious Irish significance found in a quick search through the class lists.

BJ 1 Kew Observatory Correspondence and Papers, 1851–1921. These include *BJ 1/278*, correspondence with Valencia Observatory, Co. Kerry, 1921–3.

BJ 3 Correspondence and Papers of Sir Edward Sabine, 1825–77. *BJ 3/7–13* are correspondence between Sabine and Dr Humphrey Lloyd of Trinity College, Dublin, 1833–48. *BJ 3/14–15* contain papers and reports of experiments conducted by Lloyd, with memoranda submitted by Sabine and Lloyd to the Magnetic Committee of the British Association for the Advancement of Science.

BJ 5 Meteorological Office Administrative Records, from 1910. *BJ 5/35* and 75 relate to a meteorological service for the Irish Free State, 1930–8 and 1940–6. *BJ 5/58* deals with the transfer of Shannon Airport to the government of Eire, 1938–41.

BT: *Records of the Board of Trade, its sub-departments and successor*
The Board of Trade originated in the 17th century as a committee of the Privy Council to advise the Crown on trade matters and until it merged in 1970 with the Ministry of Technology to form the Department of Trade and Industry, it was still so constituted. The records of the Lords Commissioners for Trade and Plantations (i.e. colonies) of the late 17th and most of the 18th centuries have become merged, for the most part, with those of the Colonial Office in *CO* classes (see below). They oversaw Irish trade and most Irish business dealt with by them can best be traced in the printed *Journals of the Board of Trade and Plantations*, 1704–82 (London, HMSO, 1920–38, reprinted in the Kraus reprints series by Kraus-Thomson Organisation Ltd) and in the *Calendar of State Papers Colonial*, 1675–1704 (London, HMSO, 1894–1914, also available in the Kraus reprints series). The Board of Trade was reconstituted in the 1780s and in the 19th century took on a great number of new functions relating to trade, industry and commerce. Its business touched in so many ways upon the lives of private individuals and firms that records relating to Irish people and Irish undertakings and institutions are likely to appear in many different classes.

No. XXVI in the series of PRO *Lists and Indexes* and no. XI in the supplementary series (London, HMSO, 1921 and 1980, both sets available in the Kraus reprints series) list all Board of Trade records to 1913 and selected later ones. Records of the Harbour and Marine Departments of the Board of Trade have been placed in *MT* classes (see below). The following *BT* classes are particularly well worth noting:

BT 1 General In-Letters and Files, 1791–1863. Maps and plans extracted from this class are in *BT.9* but they include none relating to Ireland; subject indexes are in *BT 19* and other registers and indexes in *BT 4*. There is a descriptive list on the PRO reference room shelves of correspondence relating to charters, licenses and letters patent from 1833 onwards, and this reveals a quantity of Irish business. *BT 1/479* (1849–50), for example, contains settlement deeds of the Irish Amelioration Society and papers on the adoption of one of the harbours of Ireland as a place of embarkation for

America; *BT 1/544* is devoted to consideration of a charter for the English and Irish Magnetic Telegraph Company in 1857; and *BT 1/547* includes papers on the Irish Institution and the Art Union of Ireland in 1858.

BT 3 General Out-Letters, 1786–1863. Each volume is indexed.

BT 4 General Registers and Indexes, 1808–64. These relate to *BT 1* and 6.

BT 6 Miscellanea, 1697–1921. These papers, to which there are some indexes and registers in *BT 4*, and some within the class itself, include several volumes relating to Irish customs and the corn supply in Ireland, 1784–92.

BT 11 Commercial Department Correspondence and Papers, from 1866. The great bulk of these papers date from 1914. A quantity of material on trading relations with Ireland is included under the subject heading of Commonwealth Trade. The class list also includes the headings Irish Free State, Irish Republic and Northern Ireland. Some indexes and registers are in *BT 35* for the period 1897–1918.

BT 12 Commercial Department Out-Letters, 1864–1921. Indexed within each volume to 1885 and in *BT 36* for the years 1897–1908.

BT 31 Companies Registration Office, Dissolved Companies, from 1856. A separate office in Dublin registered Irish companies from 1850, but English companies with Irish branches were registered in London and show up in these records. Other records of the Companies Registration Office are in *BT 34* and *41*.

BT 34 Companies Registration Office, Dissolved Companies, Liquidators' Accounts, 1890–1932. See also above, *BT 31*, and below, *BT 41*.

BT 35 Commercial Department Indexes and Registers of Correspondence, 1897–1918. They relate to papers in *BT 11*.

BT 36 Commercial Department Indexes to Out-Letters, 1897–1908.

BT 41 Companies Registration Office, Files of Joint Stock Companies Registered under the 1844 and 1856 Acts, 1844–*c.* 1860. The class contains the files for the period 1844–*c.*1860 of joint stock companies which were registered under the Act of 1844 and dissolved before 1856, and of those re-registered under the 1856 Act. For companies surviving after 1860, see *BT 31*. Irish Companies (i.e. those with head offices in Ireland) were registered in Dublin from 1850, and so do not appear in these records. Files of English companies with Irish branches will be found here, however. See also *BT 34*.

BT 42–53 Patent Office, Representations and Registers of Designs, *c.* 1840–1910. These records were created under the terms of various Acts dealing with the copyright, designs, patents and trade marks passed between 1839 and 1907, beginning with fabric designs but rapidly extended to include any manufactured article. Designs registered by Irish manufacturers etc. for copyright in Britain will be found among the rest. A detailed explanatory note on the legislative and adminstrative background of designs registration prefaces the class list in the reference room at the PRO, Kew, and the records and their provenance are also described at some length in the current *Guide*, parts I and II, and in the published *Guide to the Contents of the Public Record Office*, vol. II. Further registers and indexes of patents and trade marks are in *BT 900*. A PRO leaflet on designs and trade marks is available free of charge.

BT 55 Records of Departmental Committees, 1910–39. The committees concerned covered a very wide range of different sorts of manufacture, as well as subjects applicable to industry and commerce in general. Reference to Ireland will be found in many parts of this class. One example is *BT 55/29–31*, the records of the Flax Control Board, 1916–24, which had an Irish sub-committee.

BT 64 Industries and Manufactures Department Correspondence and Papers, from 1919. This department of the Board of Trade was established in 1918 to promote and assist home trade. It became responsible for a very wide range of work affecting industry, especially during the Second World War when it administered many war time controls. There are few records from before 1931 in this otherwise prolific class. References to industry in Ireland will be found throughout, and the subject headings under which the class is arranged include one for the Irish Republic and one for Northern Ireland.

BT 107–30, 138–45, 162–5 and 167 Records of the Registrar-General of Shipping and Seamen, from 1786, with Miscellanea (*BT 167*) from 1702. These records contain information about many individual seamen after 1835 (and some before) and about all British merchant vessels registered after 1814, as well as giving a very detailed picture of the merchant shipping industry. Their value as a potential source for Irish history is mainly genealogical. A PRO leaflet describing them is available free of charge.

BT 185 Papers of the International Beef Conference, 1937–9. The Republic of Ireland's participation in this conference is reflected here.

BT 188 Papers of the Imperial Shipping Committee, from 1920. The Republic of Ireland was represented in this committee (renamed the Commonwealth Shipping Committee in 1948) from 1926.

BT 212 Survey of Rights to Wreckage under the Merchant Shipping Act, 1854. These records, dated 1855–72, consist mainly of copies of royal grants of manorial rights, together with maps, abstracts of title and supplementary material including correspondence. The bulk of the class relates to Ireland and is listed by counties. Potentially a very rich source for the history of coastal landholding in Ireland, the documents copied for the purposes of this survey date back to the reign of Henry VIII.

BT 900 Specimens of Classes of Documents Destroyed, from 1849. The class includes registers and indexes of patents and trade marks for various dates between 1849 and 1935, which supplement the Patent Office records in *BT 42–53* (see above).

C: Records of Chancery

(NOTE: Kept at the PRO, Chancery Lane)

There is a wealth of material to be found for the mediaeval and early modern history of Ireland among the Close, Charter and Patent Rolls and other records of Chancery. These are described, with references to the many published calendars, lists, etc., in the *Guide to the Contents of the Public Record Office*, vol. I, and in M.S. Giuseppi, *Guide to the Manuscripts Preserved in the Public Record Office* (2 vols. London, HMSO, 1923–4), vol. I. For the modern period, attention should be drawn to the following classes:

C 78 Chancery Decree Rolls, 1534–1903.

C 79 Chancery Decree Rolls, Supplementary Series, 1534–20th century. This and the main series in *C 78* include decrees and orders of the Court of Chancery of Ireland, the Encumbered Estates Court of Ireland and other Irish courts.

C 183 Orders in Council (Crown Office), 1703–1891. Bundles 1 and 2 of this class contain signed and sealed copies of orders for commissions to give the royal assent to Irish Acts of Parliament, 1703–1800.

C103–14 Chancery Masters' Exhibits. They consist of title deeds, court rolls, accounts, journals, ledgers, and other documents produced before the Masters in Chancery and remaining unclaimed. They are arranged by suit under the names of Masters.* Amongst this rich and miscellaneous treasure trove some Irish material lies buried, e.g. *C 110, box 46*, which contains a large collection of papers of Oliver St. George relating to Roscommon, Leitrim, Galway, Limerick and Leix, with reference also to the estate of Thomas Knox of Dungannon and many letters (1723–30) of Owen Fallagher, agent for St. George.

CAB: Records of the Cabinet Office and Committee of Imperial Defence.
Since the Cabinet is ultimately responsible for formulating and directing all government policy, the affairs of Ireland may be expected to appear in many different classes of its records. Before the establishment of a Cabinet Secretariat in 1916, surviving records of the Cabinet are relatively sparse. From 1916 specific discussions of policy in the full Cabinet should be sought in the minutes (*CAB 23* to *1939, CAB 65* for 1939–45 and *CAB 128* from 1945) and memoranda (*CAB 24, 66–8* and *120*), which are arranged chronologically with annual indexes. An index to the subject matter of Cabinet committees, whose papers are arranged in various classes, is kept with the class list to *CAB 1* in the reference room at Kew. It includes sub-committees of the Committee of Imperial Defence, which existed as a permanent body chaired by the Prime Minister and dealing with defence policy from 1904 until 1939, though in abeyance for most of the First World War. Six PRO Handbooks deal with *CAB* records: no. 4, *List of Cabinet*

---

* Those for Rose (*C 112*, 97 bundles) being unavailable because the class still awaits listing.

Papers, 1880–1914 (London, HMSO, 1964); no. 6, *List of Papers of the Committee of Imperial Defence to 1914* (HMSO, 1964); no. 9, *List of Cabinet Papers, 1915 and 1916* (HMSO, 1966); no 11, *The Records of the Cabinet Office to 1922* (HMSO, 1966); no. 15, *The Second World War: A Guide to Documents in the Public Record Office* (HMSO, 1972); and no. 17, *The Cabinet Office to 1945* (HMSO, 1975).

CAB 1 Miscellaneous Records, 1866–1949. Mainly prior to 1920, they include scattered references to Ireland. *CAB 1/46* is a volume of documents on the Commonwealth relationship with Eire, 1948–9. Photographic copies of the bulk of papers in this class, which consists mainly of papers circulated to ministers for information, are in *CAB 37* and *42*.

CAB 2 Minutes of the Committee of Imperial Defence, 1902–39. They touch on the strategic position of Ireland from time to time.

CAB 3 Memoranda of the Committee of Imperial Defence, 1901–39. They include occasional references to Ireland.

CAB 12 Committee of Imperial Defence, Home Ports Defence Committee and Home Defence Committee, Minutes, 1909–39. They occasionally touch on the strategic position of Ireland.

CAB 13 Committee of Imperial Defence, Home Ports Defence Committee and Home Defence Committee, Memoranda and Sub-Committees, 1909–39.

CAB 16 Cabinet Ad Hoc Sub-Committees, 1905–39. *CAB 16/42* contains the proceedings and memoranda of the sub-committee on Ireland, 1922; *CAB 16/70* deals with the Irish Treaty, article 6, 1926; and piece 81 contains papers of the Irish section of the belligerent rights sub-committee, 1929.

CAB 21 Registered Files, from 1916. The class, which includes files relating to Ireland from 1920, is one of the largest of all classes of Cabinet Office records, containing the background working files to most of the decisions recorded in the minutes and memoranda in *CAB 23–4*.

CAB 27 Committees, General Series to 1939, 1915–39. The class contains minutes and papers of the bulk of Cabinet committees on Ireland before the Second World War. The subject matter is indexed at the front of the list of *CAB 1* in the reference room at Kew.

CAB 37 Photographic Copies of Cabinet Papers, 1880–1916. Memoranda circulated to the Cabinet, collected from various sources outside the PRO and including papers on·Irish policy.

CAB 41 Photographic Copies of Cabinet Letters in the Royal Archives, 1868–1916. Letters relating to Ireland will be found scattered throughout this class, which consists of letters from the Prime Minister to the Sovereign reporting Cabinet meetings, and which constitutes the most complete record of the business of the Cabinet before it became the rule in 1916 for records to be kept by the Cabinet Office rather than as personal records by ministers themselves. The class is arranged chronologically and a description of the subject matter of each letter appears in the class list in the reference room at Kew. *CAB 41/1*, for example, consisting of 53 letters dated 1868–9, includes 17 specifically dealing with Ireland, mainly on the Irish church but also covering such subjects as Irish land tenure.

CAB 42 Photographic Copies of Papers of the War Council, Dardanelles Committee and War Committee, 1914–16. Scattered references to Ireland in this class include notes on the rebellion in Ireland in 1916, in *CAB 42/12*.

CAB 43 Conferences on Ireland, 1921–2. Minutes and memoranda of meetings of British representatives and of joint meetings with represeⁿtatives of Northern and Southern Ireland. Some related files are in *CAB 21*.

CAB 61 Records of the Irish Boundary Commission, 1924–5. These include a numerical census, with names of heads of households, of Castelderg, Clogher and Dungannon Unions and Omagh Urban District.

CAB 64 Registered Files of the Minister for Co-ordination of Defence, 1924–39. The class includes the papers of the Irish Situation Committee.

CAB 104 Supplementary Registered Files, 1923–51. Originally retained by the Cabinet Office because of their security classification, the files supplement those in *CAB 21*. *CAB 104/20–4* deal mainly with defence questions affecting Ireland.

CAB 117 Reconstruction Secretariat Files, 1940–4. Among the many files in this class on all aspects of planning for post-war reconstruction is one (*CAB 117/250*) entitled 'Exchange of information with the Northern Ireland government on post-war reconstruction.'

CAB 120 Minister of Defence, Secretariat Files, 1938–47. Files of the military secretariat of the Cabinet Office for the period when Churchill and Attlee successively combined the offices of Prime Minister and Minister of Defence, with some files of earlier and later date. *CAB 120/506–7* relate to Eire and *CAB 120/582* to Northern Ireland.

CO: Records of the Colonial Office
As a result of the constitutional changes of 1920–2, responsibility for communications with the Irish Free State passed to the Colonial Office, where it was discharged first by an Irish Branch (direct successor to the Irish Office) and then to the Dominions Office in 1925. The Colonial Office thus inherited a number of records of the Irish Office and some of Dublin Castle, though most of the latter were taken over by the new Irish administration. These inherited records were subsequently transferred to the PRO under *CO* numbers; see *CO 697–9, 761–2, 903–4* and *906*, below, while a number of classes of records created by the Irish Branch and Dominions Division (later Dominions Office) responsibility also have *CO* classification; see *CO 739*,

783–5. In addition to these classes bearing directly on the administration of Ireland, material relevant to Irish history may be found in various *CO* classes bearing on emigration and on the transportation of convicts to the colonies, while Irish individuals serving in colonial administration at home and abroad may be traced throughout the *CO* records.

CO 201 Original Correspondence, New South Wales, 1783–1900 (including Tasmania to 1825). Many Irish convicts were transported to British colonies from both Irish and English ports. Their subsequent fate can often be traced, both through Home Office Records (see under *HO*, below) and through records relating to the colonies to which they were transported. *CO 201* contains detailed reports on convicts in the governors' despatches, and a report of commissioners of enquiry into the state of the colony in 1822 which contains a great deal of information on convicts.

CO 207 New South Wales Entry Books relating to Convicts, 1788–1868. They are available on microfilm at the PRO, the originals having been presented to the State Archives of New South Wales. A useful analysis of the origins of convicts from the British Isles, with a separate chapter on Ireland, is in A.G.L. Shaw, *Convicts and the Colonies* (London, 1966).

CO 384 Original Correspondence relating to Emigration and Settlement in North America, Australia, the West Indies, etc., 1817–96. Pieces 12–13, 16 and 22 are listed as specifically dealing with Irish emigrants; Hayes, *Guide to the Sources for Irish Civilisation*, cites piece 86 as containing references to Irish individuals, and there will be others in other pieces within the class.

CO 385–6 contain respectively entry books and registers relating to the correspondence in *CO 384.*

CO 532 Dominions Original Correspondence, 1907–25. The class includes correspondence concerning the Irish Free State, continued after 1925 in *DO 35* (see below).

CO 697–9 The contents of these classes, which are mentioned in Hayes's *Guide* (cited above) have now been redistributed as appropriate amongst the new classes *CO 903–4* and *906* (for which see below). They used to contain respectively Irish crimes records, Irish Office papers and registers of Irish crimes records.

CO 739 Irish Free State Original Correspondence, 1922–4. This important class consists of twenty-seven volumes of official correspondence and papers arranged under administrative headings such as 'Government of Northern Ireland', 'Government of Southern Ireland', 'Offices: Admiralty etc.', 'Individuals', and so on. Registers of correspondence and out-letters are in *CO 783–4.* Continued in *DO 3* and *35.*

CO 761 Formerly Ireland Criminal Injuries Registers; now like the contents of *CO 697–8* (above), redistributed, but in this case to *CO 905–6.*

CO 762 Ireland Criminal Injuries – Irish Grants Committee Files and Minutes, 1922–30. Until 1923 the Irish Grants Committee was known as the Irish Distress Committee. The registers and indexes to this class are in *CO 905*, and an introductory note to *CO 905* explains the statutory and administrative background to the records in both classes.

CO 783 Irish Free State Register of Correspondence, 1922–3. See *CO 739*, above.

CO 784 Irish Free State Register of Out-Letters, 1920–6. See *CO 739*, above.

CO 785 Irish Free State, *Dublin Gazettes*, 1923–5. Five volumes, continued in *DO 37* (see below).

CO 903 Ireland, Confidential Print, 1885–1919. The term 'confidential print' describes material compiled, printed and circulated within a government department for the information and consideration of various officials. Although printed, its circulation was often very strictly limited and the information it contained could be highly secret. In this class, the first two volumes deal mainly with disturbances arising out of religious intolerance. The remaining pieces contain comprehensive reports on the activities of the United Irish League from the date of its foundation in 1898, and of the Sinn Fein movement which became prominent in 1905 when the League's influence began to wane.

CO 904 Ireland, Dublin Castle Records, 1795–1926. Most of these records related to the civil and military authorities' struggle against nationalist and unionist organisations, although there are also a few papers on routine civil administration, and most departments of government in both Ireland and England seem to have corresponded with the Chief Secretary's Office in Dublin Castle at one time or another. A large proportion of the class consists of police reports, 1892–1921, and pieces 193–216 contain files on leading Irish personalities involved in the struggles for independence from 1899 to 1921, arranged alphabetically and by date. Other records kept by the British administration at its headquarters in Dublin Castle from 1782 to 1851 are in *HO 100* (see below).

CO 905 Ireland, Claims for Compensation Registers, Indexes, etc., 1922–50. These are mainly registers to the papers in *CO 762* (see above) but also include some corresondence with the Treasury.

CO 906 Irish Office Records, 1796–1924. Records of the London end of British administration of Ireland. Most of the later papers relate to the disturbances surrounding the Irish struggle for independence. The bulk of this class is drawn from the superseded classes *CO 572, 697–8* and *761*, but pieces 23–31 consist of the papers of S.G. Tallents who was sent to investigate conditions in Northern Ireland in 1922.

CP: Records of the Court of Common Pleas
(NOTE: Kept at the PRO, Chancery Lane)
They are described in detail in the *Guide to the Contents of the Public Record Office*, vol. I. The court had no Irish jurisdiction, but its records will be found to include those of proceedings involving Irish people in England. Under the Judicature Act, 1873, the Court of Common Pleas ceased to exist separately and became a division of the High Court of Justice. By Order in Council in 1880 the Common Pleas and Queen's Bench Divisions were amalgamated. Records of the Common Pleas Division between 1875 and 1880 are to be found with the other records of the Supreme Court of Judicature (see under *J*, below).

CRES: Records of the Crown Estate Commission and its predecessors
(NOTE: Kept at the PRO, Chancery Lane)
The Crown Estate Commissioners (known from 1923 to 1956 as the Commissioners of Crown Lands) have been responsible since the early 19th century for the administration of lands in England, Scotland, Wales and Ireland which the Crown has surrendered to Parliament under a succession of Civil List Acts. Their records are complementary to those of the Office of Land Revenue Receipts and Enrolments (see *LRRO* below) which also dealt with public lands. A certain amount of material relating to forest, lands and foreshores in Ireland will be found in both *CRES* and *LRRO* classes.

CRES 2 Unfiled Correspondence and Papers, 1513–1913. Papers accumulated in the Office of Woods, Forests and Land Revenues, and later transferred to the Crown Estate Commission. They are arranged under county headings and include a fair amount on Irish lands and properties.

CRES 3 Files relating to Staff and Establishment Matters, from 1731. Some concern the Quit Rent Office in Dublin.

CRES 10 Foreshores Letter Books and Treasury Report Books, 1860–1913. The class includes material on Irish foreshores.

CRES 34 Registered Files, Old Estates. The class deals with estates and manors of the Crown in England and Ireland which had been sold by 31 December 1940. Pieces 330–7 are devoted to estates in Ireland between 1834 and 1923.

CRES 36 Crown Lands, Registered Files, Establishment, Finance and General, 1743–1967. A few of these files deal with various Irish matters.

CRES 37 Registered Files, Foreshores, 1815–1969. Ireland included.

CRES 38 Title Deeds, etc., reign of Edward I to 1967. Conveyances, deeds, leases and other documents which passed to the Crown when the properties concerned (including Irish ones) were acquired. Similar documents deposited in the Land Revenue Record Office are *LRRO 5*.

CRES 40 Miscellaneous Books, 1570–1961. Accounts, letter books, etc. of the Commissioners of Woods, Forests and Land Revenues.

CRES 42 Board of Trade, Foreshores Files, 1920–35. Records of the Mercantile Marine Departments of the Board of Trade, which passed to the Commissioners of Crown Lands in 1950 when responsibility for foreshores returned to them.

CRIM: Records of the Central Criminal Court
(NOTE: Kept at the PRO, Chancery Lane)
The records of the Central Criminal Court, established in 1834 and better known as the Old Bailey, are distributed among several different repositories in the London area. Some are still kept at the Old Bailey itself, some formerly kept by the Middlesex Record Office have now been transferred to the Greater London Record Office, and others will be found at the PRO, Kew, among Home Office and Prison Commission records (see *HO 16* and *PCOM 1*, below)

CRIM 1 Depositions at the Central Criminal Court, 1839–1922. They relate to trials for murder, sedition, treason, riot and political conspiracies, and include some cases involving Irish defendants.

CSC: Records of the Civil Service Commission
The Civil Service Commission was established in 1855 to supervise appointments to all parts of the Civil Service. The nine classes of its records contain scattered references to appointments in Irish government departments and institutions, and from 1922 to the civil service of Northern Ireland. See in particular:

CSC 2 Volumes, 1853–94. Correspondence of the commission relating to all aspects of its work.

CSC 3 Files, Series I, 1875–1938. An alphabetical index to this class and *CSC 5*, arranged under various general headings, is kept in the reference room at the PRO, Kew.

CSC 4 Annual Reports, from 1855.

CSC 5 Files, Series II, from 1888. See *CSC 3* above.

CSC 8 Commissioners' Minute Books, from 1835. Some of the earlier volumes in this class include the names of candidates for employment in the Civil Service and a record of certificates of qualification.

CUST: Records of the Boards of Customs, Excise and Customs and Excise
The UK customs records, formerly divided between the Public Record

Office and Customs House, are now kept together in the PRO, Kew. They include a great deal of material directly relating to Ireland, much of it embedded among records dealing with other parts of the United Kingdom as well. For example, *CUST 9*, ledgers of exports of British merchandise, under articles, 1812–99, gives figures for the export of Irish linen yarn and other Irish merchandise. The most concentrated and most readily identified Irish material is in the following classes:

CUST 1 Minutes (Ireland), 1716–1830. (The first twelve and several later volumes of the series are missing). The class contains minutes of the proceedings of, successively, the Irish Revenue Commissioners, Irish Board of Customs and assistant commissioners of customs in Ireland. This long and highly detailed series is a particularly valuable source for the social and economic history of Ireland before 1830.

CUST 15 Ledgers of Imports and Exports: Ireland, 1698–1829. These returns, arranged under the separate importing and exporting countries, give the total values of imports and exports in each year together with their mean value during the year. There are separate returns for each Irish port until 1819 and for 1825–9 a duplicate series within the class, arranged alphabetically under the articles imported or exported.

CUST 17 States of Navigation, Commerce and Revenue, 1772–1808. these yearly statistical tables compiled by the Inspector General of Imports and Exports give detailed information over a wide range of subject matter within the broad topics of shipping, imports and exports, and customs and excise revenue, and include Irish data.

CUST 20 Salary Books and Establishments (Ireland), 1764–1826. Salary books of the revenue establishment in Ireland, each volume with alphabetical index of names.

CUST 21 Miscellaneous Books, 1715–1857. They include entry books of seizures and of letters and reports received and sent, which ought to be worth searching for Irish material. Note especially *CUST 21/17–19* which are entry books of documents relating to the new customs house at Dublin, 1771–81, to the new dock at Waterford, 1819–23 and to the rebuilding of Dublin docks, 1823–4.

CUST 22–7 These classes consist of abstracts of imports and exports from the 1870s to 1899, arranged separately under ports and articles, with one class (*CUST 27*) of transhipments of dutiable imports and exports, 1884–99. All include references to Irish trade.

CUST 30 Board and Secretariat Out-Letter Entry Books, Extra-Departmental, 1812–1900. These include some in-letters as well. They are arranged under various subject headings including one for Privy Council and Treasury, Irish and Scottish affairs, 1824–48.

CUST 31 Out-Letter Entry Books, Interdepartmental, 1700–1900. These include letters from the Board of Customs to Ireland, 1822–82.

CUST 32 Board and Secretariat In-Letter Books, Extra- and Intra-Departmental, 1707–1882. A considerable amount of Irish material is contained in this class under various headings, all between 1823 and 1875.

CUST 36 Statistics, Trade and Shipping, 1699–1828. These records of the Board of Customs include details of imports and exports to Ireland between 1699 and 1766 and to Great Britain as a whole from 1708 to 1784. Two volumes on shipping, 1799–1800 and 1814–28, will also contain Irish material.

CUST 38 Statistics, Establishments, 1782–1812. The class includes material on salaries and staffs at outports and in the coastguard in Ireland.

CUST 39 Establishment, Staff Lists, 1671–1922. Details of staff employed by the Board of Customs specifically in Ireland appear in pieces 122–44 and 161–2. These records, however, are closed for 100 years, and some relate to times within the restricted period.

CUST 40 Establishment, General, 1818–1926. This class includes one piece (*CUST 40/30*) relating to the Irish gauger Patrick O'Connor, a dubious character whose murderers were executed publicly in 1849.

CUST 41 Legal, Copies of Counsels' Opinions, 1701–1849. Pieces 39–41 relate to customs property in Ireland, 1833–49, piece 41 being a schedule of deeds dated 1628–1831.

CUST 42 Customs, Other Headquarters Departments, 1716–1902. This class includes a Comptroller-General's precedent book for Scotland and Ireland, 1826–78 and two volumes dealing with the Irish Charity Fund and Dublin Coal Fund between 1853 and 1902.

CUST 47 Excise Board and Secretariat Minute Books, 1695–1867. These indexed volumes, mainly relating to appointments and including minutes of the Board of Inland Revenue from 1849, include references to employees in Ireland.

CUST 50–101, 103 Outport Records, 17th–20th centuries. The principal business of outports, i.e. all those ports other than the Port of London around the coast of England and Wales, is to receive and account for payment of customs and other duties. The outport records therefore will be found to contain material relating to Irish trade with England and Wales, although this is not always easy to separate from the rest. The records are arranged in classes for each outport (with a few small ones grouped together) and the majority of volumes are individually indexed. For outport records specifically relating to Ireland, see below, *CUST 113*.

CUST 103 Excise Trials, 1778–1847. Court proceedings including Irish cases, 1830–47.

CUST 110 Irish Board and Establishment, Minutes and Appointments, 1824–33. These are records of the board of commissioners appointed to transact excise business in Ireland under the Customs and Excise Act, 1823.

CUST 111 Irish Revenue Police Records, 1830–57. These concern appointments, etc. to the revenue police force which was reorganised in 1830 to combat the illicit making of malt and distillation of spirits in contravention of the Irish (Illicit Distillation (Ireland)) Act, 1831.

CUST 112 Irish Revenue Board and Irish Board of Customs, Entry Books, 1744–1828. These relate to orders and regulations concerning customs and excise duties, with solicitors' reports, 1744–7, and excise statistics, 1746–1822.

CUST 113 Outport Records, Ireland, 1679–1849.

D: Records of the Development Commission
The Development Commission is a body of eight commissioners administering the Development Fund under the terms of the Development and Road Improvement Funds Acts, 1909 and 1910. Its functions have changed considerably during its existence, but in very general terms it has always been concerned with assisting agriculture, rural industries and the fisheries. There is a small amount of Irish material.

D 4 Correspondence and Papers of the Commission, from 1910. *D 4/48–9* deal with the Development Fund and the Government of Ireland Act. Minutes, reports to the Treasury, printed annual reports and official notices are to be found in *D 1*, *D 2*, *D 3*, and *D 5* respectively.

DO: Records of the Dominions Office and the Commonwealth Relations Office
The Dominions Office was established in 1925 and renamed the Commonwealth Relations Office in 1947, just before the transfer of power in India. From its foundation it was responsible for the conduct of relations between the UK and the Irish Free State (subsequently Irish Republic, then Eire), taking over that responsibility from the Dominions Division of the Colonial Office. Records in *DO* classes are therefore an important source both for the history of relations between the Irish Republic and Great Britain and for that of Irish relations with the Commonwealth.

DO 35 Dominions Original Correspondence, from 1926. The class, which includes papers on the Irish Free State, and subsequently on Eire, continues from *CO 532* (see above). From 1929 the registers in *DO 3* are an essential finding aid. Supplementary correspondence is in *DO 117* (continued from *CO 739*).

DO 37 Irish Free State, *Dublin Gazettes*, 1926–55. Continued from *CO 785*. They are open without restriction, not subject to the thirty-year rule.

DO 99 Irish Free State Sessional Papers, 1922–56. Also open without restriction as to date.

DO 100 Irish Free State Miscellanea, 1925–52. Ten volumes of trade and shipping statistics and statistical abstracts, all open without restiction as to date.

DO 114 Confidental Print, Dominions, 1924–51. (For a definition of confidential print, see *CO 903*, above). This class covers a wide range of business relating to the Dominions, with a small amount on Ireland.

DO 117 Supplementary Original Correspondence, 1926–9. The records in this class were orignally held back because of their security classification, and some are still closed for 50 or 100 years. They supplement those in *DO 35* and should also be used by reference to the registers in *DO 3*.

DO 118 Agreements, Treaties and Miscellaneous Documents, 1856–1965. These are the British government's copies of formal documents relating to agreements, treaties, etc., with or relating to various Commonwealth countries and Ireland.

DO 121 Private Office Papers, 1924–50. Unregistered files which used to be held in the Private Office of the Dominions (later Commonwealth Relations) Office. They cover a wide range of subjects, and have been arranged in general subject groups followed by headings for each of the Commonwealth countries. Much of the class is subject to extended closure for various periods, and there is as yet very little Irish material available.

DO 130 UK representative to Eire, Archives and Correspondence, 1939–47. Eighty-seven files of correspondence of the UK representative primarily with the Dominions Office and the Irish department of External Affairs. They are listed chronologically, with file titles also given.

DPP: Records of the Director of Public Prosecutions
(NOTE: Kept at the PRO, Chancery Lane)
Records of the prosecution of individual Irish people in British courts will be found amongst the papers of the Director of Public Prosecutions, but the majority of these are closed for period of 75 or 100 years on grounds of personal sensitivity.

DPP 1 Case papers: Old Series, 1889–1830. Closed for 75 years.

DPP 3 Registers of Cases, 1884–1951. Closed for 75 years.

DPP 4 Transcripts of Proceedings, 1846–1931.

DSIR: Records of the Department of Scientific and Industrial Research and its successors

The Department of Scientific and Industrial Research, created in 1916 and abolished in 1965, both inherited and has passed on to other departments responsibility for an extrememely diverse range of government involvement in research. Any involvement with Ireland was purely incidental to its functions, but the following examples suggest possible areas of investigation among *DSIR* records.

DSIR 4 Building Research: Correspondence and Papers, from 1919. *DSIR 4/2405* is a file on investigations of natural lighting in the Royal Courts of Justice, Belfast; *DSIR 4/2406* contains the report of an investigation of acoustics in the House of Commons and Senate Chambers at Stormont; *DSIR 4/2481* is a report on cleaning the stonework of Newry Town Hall.

DSIR 8 Fuel Research Board Papers, from 1915. These include papers of the Irish Peat Enquiry Committee, 1917–22.

DSIR 9 Geological Survey Board Papers, from 1853. The Geological Survey Board was responsible for the Geological Survey of Ireland from 1845 until 1905, when this responsibility was transferred to the Department of Agriculture and Technical Instruction for Ireland. In 1947 a branch office for the Geological Survey Board opened in Belfast to undertake a survey of Northern Ireland. A number of papers in this class relate wholly or in part to Ireland.

DSIR 13 Water Pollution Research Board Papers, from 1920. *DSIR 13/365–72* contain correspondence with the government of Northern Ireland relating to various aspects of water pollution, and a few other files in the class have some relevance to Ireland.

E: Records of the Exchequer

(NOTE: Kept at the PRO, Chancery Lane)

As in the case of the Chancery records, those of the Exchequer constitute a rich source for the mediaeval and early modern history of Ireland. They are described, with references to the many printed lists, indexes, etc., in the *Guides* to the Public Records cited above. For the modern period the following are worthy of note:

E 403 Enrolments and Registers of Issues, reign of Henry III to 1834. Some relate to Ireland, e.g. Irish civil list establishment papers, 1809–15.

E 407 Exchequer of Receipt, Miscellaneous Books and Papers. The class includes *E 407/12–15*, accounts and papers on the expenses of troops in England, Ireland and abroad, 1559–1777.

E 408 Records of the Comptroller-General of the Exchequer. A quantity deal with Ireland, 1837–67.

NOTE: For records of the Office of the Auditors of Land Revenue, a subsidiary of the Exchequer, see *LR*, below.

ED: Records of Education Departments

ED 24 Private Office Papers, 1851–1935. They include two files (pieces 1347–8) on education in Ireland.

ED 28 Science and Art Department Minute Books, 1852–76. Until about 1865 the responsibilities of the Science and Art Department of the Board of Education included the Museum of Irish Industry and the Royal Dublin Society.

FO: Records of the Foreign Office and Foreign and Commonwealth Office

Most classes within this very large group fall into a few clear cut categories:
  i)   General Correspondence (political, diplomatic, commercial, consular, treaty, etc.). Correspondence of the Foreign Office with its representatives abroad, foreign representatives in London, other government departments, and private individuals or associations. Until 1906 this is arranged on a country basis, with one class (occasionally two) for each country; thereafter a few broad functional classes (political, commercial, library) replace the country classes.
  ii) Embassy and Consular Archives. Records maintained by British missions abroad, and periodically returned to the UK for safe keeping. As well as correspondence, letter books, registers, indexes, etc., forming to a degree the counterpart to the records in (i) above, these may contain consular and other court records, registers of British subjects, their births, marriages and deaths, registers of passports, land titles and shipping records.
  iii) Confidential Print. Copies of the more important despatches, minutes, etc., printed for circulation within the Foreign Office, to the Cabinet, to ministers abroad. Arranged in a numerical series (*FO 881*) and also by country, region, or subject.
  iv) Archives of Commissions and Conferences, e.g. the Reparation Commission 1919 (*FO 801*) and the Locarno Conference (*FO 840*).
  v)   Private Papers. Papers of Foreign Office officials, members of the diplomatic or consular services, etc.
References to the dealings of Irish individuals and the Irish nation will be found in many of them. Many *FO* lists are in print, and PRO handbook no. 13, *The Records of the Foreign Office 1782–1939*, is a useful guide.

FO 5 General Correspondence before 1906, United States of America Series II, 1793–1905. Forty-eight volumes on the Fenian Brotherhood in the USA between 1864 and 1897 are listed as pieces 1334–51, 1427, 1535, 1556, 1559, 1706–7, 1745–6, 1776–80, 1816–20, 1860–3, 1928–32, 1975, 2044 and 2359. *FO 5/2348* relates to a group of named Fenian 'dynamiters', 1896–7, and volumes in this class dealing with extraditions will also be worth close attention. An index to Foreign Office cases is available in the PRO reference room at Kew, and provides a guide to particular collections of subject-matter, like the volumes on Fenians in various *FO* classes. Registers to *FO* correspondence before 1906, arranged by countries, are in *FO 804* and are kept on the open shelves in the reference room at Kew. See also *FO 115*, below.

FO 95 Miscellanea, Series I, 1639–1942. This class contains some of the papers of Philippe d'Auvergne, Prince de Bouillon, and of other French aristocrats who during the period of the French Revolution and the Napoleonic Wars not only aided their fellow refugees but also acted as gatherers of information for the British government. These passed on, among much else, useful information on relations between disaffected Irish and the French and the plans of the successive French regimes to use Ireland and Irish forces against England. Other Bouillon papers are in *PC 1*, Privy Council papers, *WO 1* War Office in-letters, *HO 69*, a special class of Bouillon papers, and in a volume of Treasury miscellanea, *T 64/354*. Papers of the Comte de Calonne, which are less extensive but of a similar importance, are to be found both in this class, *FO 95* and in *PC 1*. Separate lists of both Bouillon and Calonne papers are available at the PRO, Kew and Chancery Lane, and are in the process of being improved and updated. In addition to the foregoing, some other Irish material will be found in *FO 95*, e.g. in *FO 95/575*, papers of the Comte d'Avaux (1640–1709), and in *FO 95/649*, a report and papers dated 1815 on the claim of Col John Cruise of the Austrian army to family estates in Ireland.

FO 96 Miscellanea, Series II, *c*.1700–1937. This class is not as rich a hunting ground for Irish sources as *FO 95*, the first series of Foreign Office miscellanea. It contains, however, a number of petitions, original passports, etc., which probably include those of some Irish people. Among a collection of addresses to the sovereign is one dated 1887, congratulating Queen Victoria on her golden jubilee and signed by British, Canadian, Irish and colonial residents of New York.

FO 97 Supplement to General Correspondence, 1780–1905. Pieces 472–5 consist of four volumes of confidential print on 'press incitements to outrage' in the USA, 1881–5, which complement the volumes on the Fenian Brotherhood in *FO 5*, cited above. For a definition of confidential print, see above, introductory remarks to *FO*, and under *CO 903*.

FO 115 Embassy and Consular Archives, United States of America Correspondence, 1791–1945. There are several other classes of consular correspondence emanating from the various British consulates in the USA. This one, however, contains the main embassy correspondence from Washington, and at certain times (e,g, during the First World War) a large part of its business seems to have concerned Irish-American relations and the Irish in America. Indexes to this corrrespondence between 1916 and 1929 are in *FO 951*.

NOTE: Taken together, *FO 5* and *115*, supplemented by the other classes of embassy and consular archives from British consulates in the United States of

America, form a good example of a collection of Foreign Office records well worth searching for material on Irish history. Owing to the history of Irish emigration and of Anglo-American relations, these records are almost certainly richer in such material than most others. Records dealing with other countries are well worth searching for particular cases, however; and the embassy and consular archives often provide a valuable supplement to the main series of general correspondence. For example:

FO 337 Embassy and Consular Archives, Norway Correspondence, 1905–45. *FO 337/107* deals with the activities of Sir Roger Casement in Norway in 1914–15.

FO 371 General Correspondence after 1906, Political, from 1906. The classes of general correspondence after 1906 reflect administrative rather than geographical divisions, and of these the 'political' (sometimes called 'diplomatic') contains by far the largest quantity of material. Other classes of general correspondence after 1906 are: *FO 368*, commercial, *FO 369*, consular, *FO 370*, library, and *FO 372*, treaty. Along with *FO 371*, all these classes were indexed annually together, by subject matter as well as by persons and places. From 1906 to mid 1920 the index was in card form, and is now kept in the reference room of the PRO at Kew. In 1920 the system changed to one using printed volumes. These index volumes are reprinted annually by the Kraus Thomson Organisation, as the records to which they refer become available under the thirty-year rule. Copies are available at the PRO and will also be found in university libraries and elsewhere. They provide an extremely detailed guide to the contents of 20th-century Foreign Office papers, including any business concerned with Ireland and the Irish as it touched on British foreign relations.

FO 627 General Correspondence after 1906, Dominions Information, 1929–33. These records of the Dominions Information Department of the Foreign Office deal with relations between the Dominions and other countries, and other matters falling within Foreign Office competence. Much of their contents relates to the Irish Free State. Earlier and later records of this department and its successors are in *FO 372*.

FO 944 Control Office for Germany and Austria: Finance Files. The Control Office for Germany and Austria (which became the German Section of the Foreign Office in 1947) dealt with the London end of British military government in German after the Second World War. *FO 944/186* is a file on German assets in Eire, 1947–8. Although this appears to be an isolated example of a file dealing specifically with Ireland among these records, *FO 944* and other *FO* classes of records, both of the Control Office and of the Control Commissions for Germany and Austria, would be worth searching for evidence of economic and other links between Germany and Ireland.

FS: *Records of the Registry of Friendly Societies.*
Established under the Friendly Societies Acts of 1829, 1846 and 1875, the Registry of Friendly Societies came to include the registration of buildings

and loan societies, trade unions and industrial and providence societies among its functions. From 1875 assistant registrars subordinated to the chief registrar kept registries for Scotland and Ireland. The business of local Irish societies, therefore, does not in general show up among *FS* records. National societies including Ireland among their resonsibilites were registered centrally, however, and copies of their rules, correspondence between them and the Registry, etc. are to be found here. *FS* records can also provide useful evidence on the occupations of Irish immigrants in Britain.

FS 1 Friendly Societies Rules and Amendments, Series I, *c.*1784–1875.

FS 2 Indexes to *FS 1*, *c.*1784–1875.

FS 3 Friendly Societies Rules and Amendments, Series II, 1876–1913.

FS 4 Indexes to *FS 3*, 1876–1913.

FS 5 Friendly Societies Branches Rules and Amendments, etc., Series I, 1855–1912.

FS 7 Trade Unions Rules and Amendments, etc., Series I, 1850–1912.

FS 10 Friendly Societies Branches Rules and Amendments, Series II, from 1851.

FS 11 Trade Unions Rules and Amendments, etc., Series II, from 1848.

FS 15 Amendments to Friendly Societies Rules, etc., 1793–1948.

HLG: Records of the Minstry of Housing and Local Government and its predecessors.

The great majority of functions of the successive ministries responsible for housing, local government and related duties were exercised locally in Ireland through the various organs of Irish government. *HLG* records therefore contain little relating to Ireland, except where changes of policy involved the ministry in decisions on procedure affecting Northern Ireland as well as the rest of the UK. Scattered files on administration in Northern Ireland are to be found, for example, in:

HLG 7 Records of Special Wartime Functions, 1925–54.

HO: Records of the Home Office and Ministry of Home Security

The Home Office had overall responsibility for the affairs of Ireland until 1922 and for Northern Ireland from then until 1972, when the Home Office Northern Ireland Department became part of the new Northern Ireland Office. Although most administration of Ireland before 1922 was in the hands of the Chief Secretary's Office in Dublin and the Irish Office in London, the Home Office, in addition to maintaining a general oversight of Irish affairs, also retained direct responsibility for grants, commissions and appointments, and for other civil and military affairs. The Fenian disturbances led to the appointment of an assistant on Irish affairs in 1867, and for a short time in 1916 the Home Office assumed direct control of Irish administration while there was no Chief Secretary. *HO* is the group of British public records in which perhaps the greatest concentration of Irish historical source material will be found. Apart from those classes consisting almost exclusively of the records of British administration of Ireland, the activities of Irish people in Britain are reflected in many other Home Office records. First of these in numerical order is the large collection of papers relating to criminals, *HO 6–27*, continued and supplemented in *HO 42, 44–5, 47* and *144*. For further sources on Irish convicts transported to New South Wales and Tasmania, see the introduction to *CO* records and *CO 201* and *207* above. The Home Office criminal papers are likely to be of particular interest, as far as Irish history is concerned, to the genealogist. They are arranged as follows:

HO 6 Circuit Letters, 1816–40.

HO 7 Convicts, Miscellaneous, 1785–1835.

HO 8 Convict Prisons, 1824–76.

HO 9 Convict Prisons, Miscellaneous Registers, 1802–49.

HO 10 Settlers and Convicts, New South Wales and Tasmania, 1707–1859.

HO 11 Convict Transportation Registers, 1787–1870.

HO 12 Criminal Papers, Old Series, 1849–71. They include, in *HO 12/179/81780–80A*, papers relating to the trial of Michael Barrett after the Clerkenwell explosion, 1868 (cited with slightly incomplete references in Hayes's *Guide*). Much more will be found in this class, as in the others, dealing with the prosecution of Irish individuals for crimes committed in Britain, whether with a political background or not.

HO 13 Criminal Entry Books, 1782–1871

HO 14 Registers of Criminal Papers, 1849–70.

HO 15 Criminal and Miscellaneous Warrant Books, 1850–98.

HO 16 Old Bailey Sessions, 1815–49. See also *CRIM 1*, above, and *PCOM 1*, below.

HO 17 Criminal Petitions, Series I, 1819–39.

HO 18 Criminal Petitions, Series II, 1839–54.

HO 19 Registers of Criminal Petitions, 1797–1853.

HO 20 Prisons Correspondence and Papers, 1820–43.

HO 21 Prisons Entry Books, Series I, 1812–84.

HO 22 Prisons Entry Books, Series II, 1849–21

HO 23 Registers of County Prisons, 1847–66

HO 24 Prison Registers and Returns, 1838–75

HO 25 Criminal Entry Books, Public Departments, 1850–71.

HO 26 Criminal Registers, Series I, 1791–1849.

HO 27 Criminal Registers, Series II, 1805–92.

The following *HO* classes reflect the multifarious non-criminal business of the Home Office, in which the affairs of Ireland were included:

HO 30 War and Colonial Office Correspondence, 1794–1840. In–Letters to the Home Office on matters concerning domestic and colonial defence, law and order, etc. See also *HO 50–1*

HO 40 Disturbances Correspondence, 1812–55. Reports, papers, précis of information, etc. relating to riots, disturbances and political agitation in Britain.

HO 41 Disturbances Entry Books, 1815–1916. Closed for 100 years.

HO 42 Domestic Correspondence, reign of George III, 1782–1820. Like the following two classes, this one contains material on a wide range of business, including a certain amount on Ireland.

HO 43 Domestic Entry Books, 1782–1898. From 1782 to 1871 these contain copies and/or précis of out-letters to the Lord Chancellor, judges, local magistrates and officials, police authorities and private individuals on matters of local administration and justice. There is a gap for 1871–3 (when such out-letters appear in *HO 136*) but the series then continues to 1898, after which the Home Office entered its correspondence in a number of different series dealing with particular subjects. From 1792 most volumes contain an index. The earlier volumes are indexed in *SP 44/417*.

HO 44 Domestic Correspondence, reign of George IV and later, 1820–61. These continue the series in *HO 42* and are continued in turn in *HO 45*, with which there is some overlap.

HO 45 Registered Papers, from 1839. This class, which still accrues each year, contains the main records of general Home Office business from 1839, although for the period 1839–61 there is some overlap with *HO 44*. It is arranged under subject headings including one for Ireland. From 1841 the papers in this class were registered in daily registers in *HO 46*, with criminal papers from 1849–70 being registered in *HO 14*. Business relating to Ireland in this large and important class covers a very wide range of subject matter. Examples from the early period include numerous papers on Fenians, various charters and warrants for Irish officials and institutions, files on charities, factories, famine relief, papers on the Irish Land Acts and on the Government of Ireland (Home Rule) Bill, 1892–3. Such subjects continue to appear in the class at later dates. For the period leading up to independence and partition and its ʹaftermath there is much on the Royal Irish Constabulary, on administrative changes resulting from the Government of Ireland Act, 1920, on various other Bills and Acts of Parliament relating to Ireland, on relations with the Irish Free State in matters such as passports and visas, the judiciary, relief of refugees and a multitude of other subjects. The administration of Northern Ireland is reflected also in a large quantity of files. For the period after 1878, many criminal papers, especially those relating to particular individuals, and some on other subjects regarded as being particularly sensitive, are in *HO 144* and subject to closure for 100 years, although the Home Office will consider applications to see papers 75 years old or more.

HO 46 Daily Registers, from 1841. With the exception of criminal papers for 1849–70, which were registered in *HO 14*, the registers in *HO 46* relate to all the business contained in files in *HO 45* and *144*.

HO 47 Judges' Reports, 1784–1829. Letters and reports from judges on criminal cases, including petitions for commutations of sentences, free pardons, etc.

HO 50 Military Correspondence, 1782–1840. This class deals with various matters of internal and domestic defence including law and order and militia and volunteer forces. The entry books in *HO 51* are a useful guide.

HO 51 Military Entry Books, 1758–1855. Entries of out-letters to the Secretary at War, War Department, etc. on subjects included in *HO 50*.

HO 64 Rewards and Pardons and Secret Service Papers, 1820–40. Correspondence relating to the offer of rewards and pardons for criminal information, with secret service reports, copies of seditious publications, etc.

HO 69 Bouillon Papers, 1789–1809. Original letters to the Prince de Bouillon (see above, under *FO 95*) whose activities in tracking down French republican spies and their associates brought him into contact with several Irish individuals and organisations.

HO 73 Various Commissions, 1876–94. Records of the Commission on Irish Education, 1834, are in *HO 73/33*.

HO 77 Newgate Calendar, 1782–1853. Printed lists of the prisoners to be tried at Newgate, with manuscript additions stating the results of the trials from July 1822.

HO 79 Private and Secret Entry Books, 1798–1864. Entry Books of out-letters relating to secret service and other confidential matters, postal censorship, alleged criminal acts, etc. *HO 79/6–9* deals with Ireland between 1803 and 1864. Some original correspondence dealing with the same sort of subject-matter and including references to Ireland between 1820 and 1840 is in *HO 64*, and later out-letters are in *HO 151*.

HO 89 Warrants for Patents of Inventions, Entry Books, 1783–1834. One example of many classes which might profitably be searched for dealings with Irish individuals.

HO 100 Ireland Correspondence and Papers, 1782–1851. Original correspondence and papers of the Home Office relating to Ireland, arranged chronologically and under the following headings: civil, military, private and secret, miscellaneous. In addition to these, the following special subjects appear: Catholic emancipation, 1824; peerage claims, 1828–31; poor law reform, 1836–9; reports of outrages, 1836–40; and the report of the Irish Land Commission, 1820–3. The class continues in *HO 45*.

HO 101 Ireland, King's Letter Books, 1776–1915. Entries of royal sign manual letters, warrants, etc. addressed to the Lord Lieutenant of Ireland. These very formal documents will be found duplicated in *SO 1* (see below) which starts in 1627 and contains many warrants of a financial nature not included in *HO 101*.

HO 107 Census Returns, 1841–51. (NOTE: These are kept at the PRO, Chancery Lane. Readers normally do not consult the originals, but see microfilm copies in a special reading room run by the PRO in the Land Registry building, Portugal Street, London WC2. See also under *RG* below). These are enumerators' schedules of the returns made by heads of households. They include the names, age, sex and occupation of individuals in England, Wales, the Channel Islands, and Isle of Man. In the 1841 census it is noted whether a person was born in the same county as the return or in Scotland, Ireland or elsewhere. The later 19th-century census returns are in *RG 9–11* (see below).

HO 119 Law Officers' Reports, Miscellaneous, 1792–1870. They include original Private and Secret reports (with some on Irish conspiracies) and reports on civil and criminal cases.

HO 121 Ireland, General Letter Books, 1782–1871. Entries of out-letters relating to civil and military affairs. Each volume is indexed, and there are registers of in-letters and out-letters, 1787–1801, in *HO 123*.

HO 123 Ireland, Miscellaneous Entry Books, 1768–1877.

HO 129 Ecclesiastical Census Returns, 1851. Returns of churches and chapels, endowments, sittings and estimated attendances on 30 March 1851, with average numbers during the previous twelve months. These will be of interest for research into Irish communites in England. (NOTE: These records are to be seen at Chancery Lane. See *HO 107* above, and *RG* below).

HO 133 Explosives Entry Books, 1873–1921. (Before 1873 out-letters relating to the control and inspection of explosives will be found in *HO 43* and *136*).

HO 134 Extradition Entry Books, 1873–1921. Out-letters dealing with the negotiation and implementation of extradition treaties and with commissions rogatories. These records are closed until they are 100 years old.

HO 136 Miscellaneous Entry Books, 1871–99. Until 1873, these include entries of out-letters on explosives.

HO 140 Calendars of Prisoners, 1868–1958. Lists of prisoners tried at Assizes and Quarter Sessions, with details of ages, occupations, charges, verdicts, sentences, etc. Closed for 100 years.

HO 141 Appointments, Charters, Commissioners, etc. Warrant Books, 1852–6.

HO 142 Change of Name and Arms Warrant Books, 1868–1921.

HO 144 Supplementary Registered Papers, 1868–1947. Papers on criminal and other subjects which were considered for various reasons too sensitive to release with the main series of Home Office registered papers in *HO 45*. They are closed to public inspection until they are 100 years old, although the Home Office will consider applications to see papers 75 years old or more. *HO 144/1537–8* are two boxes containing the papers of Sir Robert Anderson (1841–1918) from 1867 to 1901. Anderson was Home Office adviser in matters relating to political crime from 1868, and from 1888 was Assistant Commissioner of Police of the Metropolis and Head of the Criminal Investigation Department. He was responsible for Home Office policy relating to the Fenians.

HO 151 Confidential Entry Books, 1871–1921. Out-letters on firearms, extradition, postal censorship, criminal and other confidential matters. Closed for 100 years.

HO 152 Domestic and Industrial Entry Books, 1899–1921. Out-letters classified under various headings, including Ireland.

HO 161 Casement Diaries, 1901–11. The diaries of Sir Roger Casement, who was executed for high treason in 1916. These diaries can be seen only by special arrangement, the details of which are given in the relevant volume of PRO class lists at Kew.

HO 184 Royal Irish Constabulary Records, 1816–1922. These consist of: registers of service, 1816–1921; returns of personnel both numerical (1841–1919) and nominal (1910–21) with various other staff lists and registers;

journals of the Auxiliary Division, 1920–2; law opinions, 1874–1919; intelligence notes, 1895; circulars, financial records and miscellanea.

HO 186, 191–212, 216, 217, 220 Records of the Ministry of Home Security, 1939–45. These records are described in some detail in PRO Handbook no. 15, *The Second World War. A Guide to Documents in the Public Record Office* (London, HMSO, 1972). The ministry's responsibilities included the whole of the UK and Northern Ireland, and much of the general policy and administration recorded at the PRO relates to Northern Ireland as to all other parts of the country. For example, *HO 191/11* is a statement of civilian casualties and chronological record of air attacks in the UK and Northern Ireland resulting from enemy action from 1939 to 1945, among the unregistered papers of the ministry's Research and Experiments Department. At a regional level, however, the ministry's functions were exercised through the government of Northern Ireland, and records of World War II home security administration relating purely to Northern Ireland should be sought at the PRO of Northern Ireland in Belfast.

HO 219 Londonderry Inquiry, 1972. Proceedings and reports of the Widgery Tribunal of Inquiry into the events in Londonderry on Sunday 30 January 1972, together with photographs, maps, films and sound recordings used in evidence. The films and sound recordings are held on special deposit in the National Film Archive. These records are not subject to thirty-year closure, and may be seen without restriction.

HO 221 Royal Commission on the Constitution, 1967–73. This commission, chaired first by Lord Crowther and after his death in 1972 by Lord Kilbrandon, examined the functions of the central government and legislature in relation to the counties, nations and regions of the United Kingdom. The class consists of material submitted in evidence in various forms, research and policy papers and minutes of the commission, including much submitted by Northern Irish bodies and individuals, and/or relating to Northern Ireland. All except the policy papers and minutes are open without restriction.

HO 241 Royal Commision on Standards of Conduct in Public Life, 1974–6 (the Salmon Commission). Summaries of evidence given before this commission are included in the class and are open now. They include that given by several Northern Irish bodies.

HO 244 Committee on Broadcasting, 1960. Chaired by Sir Henry Pilkington, this committee considered broadcasting throughout the UK. Evidence in the class is open now and includes some given by Northern Irish bodies and/or bearing on Northern Ireland.

HO 245 Commmittee on the Future of Broadcasting, 1974–7. (The Annan Committee). Evidence in this class is also open now and includes Irish material.

HO 246 Northern Ireland Private Office Papers, 1924–6. Three files of correspondence between the Home Office and the secretariat in Northern Ireland on various subjects in the period immediately after the partition.

HO 248 Northern Ireland Detainees Enquiry, 1971. This class consists only of one booklet, the published report of the Committee of Inquiry into Allegations against the Security Forces of Physical Brutality in Northern Ireland arising out of the events of 9 August 1971.

HO 261 Data Protection Committee, 1976–8. Chaired by Sir Norman Lindop. The evidence before the committee is open now, and includes a small amount from Northern Irish bodies.

INF: Records of the Ministry of Information in the Second World War (with one class, *INF 4*, on information services in the First World War.) Irish material will be found among these records in a number of different guises. Home propaganda was administered on a regional basis according to centrally determined policy; and the ministry's regional divisions were coterminous with those of the Ministry of Home Security (see *HO 186*, etc., above) leaving Northern Ireland to its own local administration. The main series of correspondence files in *INF 1*, however, reflect both policy decisions affecting the whole of the UK including Northern Ireland, and some specifically Northern Irish considerations, particularly among the papers of the Religious Division. Eire was treated for most purposes as a foreign country, but within the responsibility of the Empire Division, and files on British propaganda in Eire appear under Empire Division in *INF 1*. Among the guard books of publicity material issued by the ministry (*INF 2*), however, there appears a volume of publicity for the UK *and* Eire. Material will be found throughout the *INF* classes, therefore, reflecting many different aspects of Anglo-Irish relations during the Second World War and illustrating the many and various manifestations of British war-time propaganda to which the Irish people were exposed. The Ministry of Information records for the period of the Second World War are arranged as follows:

INF 1 Files of Correspondence, 1936–50. These include material from the period immediately before the war, when the forerunner of the ministry was a department of the Home Office connected with the Foreign Office, and minutes of the Inter-Allied Information Committee (New York), 1940–3.

INF 2 Guard Books, from 1939. These include a complete set of all the printed publicity material distributed by the Ministry of Information during the war, some of it in photographic copies.

INF 3 Original Art Work, 1939–46.

INF 4 War of 1914–18 Information Services, 1915–43.

INF 5 Crown Film Unit Files, 1936–54.

INF 6 Film Production Documents, 1932–69.

INF 9 Dixon Scott Collection of Photographs. Purchased in 1948 by the Central Office of Information, as the ministry became, this collection dates approximately from the inter-war period and covers various scenes throughout the British Isles. It includes twenty-five envelopes of photographs of particular places in both Eire and Northern Ireland, and one (*INF 9/318*) entitled simply 'Irish life'.

INF 13 Posters and Publications, 1939–76. For the war period, this material is similar to and often duplicates that in *INF 2*. In some cases, however, an original copy of a poster or leaflet appears in *INF 13* whereas only a photograph was entered in the *INF 2* Guard Book.

NOTE: Various classes of *INF* records dating from later than 1946 may well be worth searching for Irish records, though none appears to be so useful as *INF 9*, described above.

IR: Records of the Board of Inland Revenue and its predecessors.

IR records include a large number of classes dealing with the survey, census and/or registration of individuals and/or their property for a wide range of taxes and other payable duties. For this reason, as with some other public record classes (military records, for instance), they are almost all worth searching for traces of individual Irish people even though in most cases the administrative purposes which gave rise to the records did not include Ireland.

IR 1 Board of Stamps Apprenticeship Books, 1710–1811. Registers of moneys received in payment of the duty on apprentices' indentures. They record the names, addresses and trades of the masters, names of the apprentices and dates of the articles. Since masters did not have to pay stamp duty on the indentures of apprentices taken on at public expense or at the charge of any charity, these books are very far from being a complete record of apprentices in Britain during the century they cover. Indexes are to be found within the classes and in *IR 17*.

IR 2 Parochial, Inspectors' and Land Tax Ledgers, 1857–1948. The ledgers show totals of income tax, inhabited house duty and land tax paid in each parish in the UK, including Ireland until 1914. Only ledgers for certain years are included.

IR 4 Lottery Books, 1780–1844. They include registers of agents and allocation of prize certificates. See also *IR 55*, below.

IR 6 Estate Duty Office Letters, 1812–36.

IR 8 Land Tax Redemption Registers, 1863–1914. See *IR 20–5*, below.

IR 12 Assessed Taxes Cases, 1823–58. Points on assessed taxes determined by judges, with indexes.

IR 13 Board of Taxes, Treasury Guard Books, 1797–1900. Entry book of correspondence with the Treasury on the administration of various taxes, including staff matters.

IR 15 Commissioner of Inland Revenue Annual Reports, from 1856. Open without restriction.

IR 16 Tax Abstracts and Statistics, 1845–1912. They include those compiled for Ireland.

IR 17 Indexes to Apprenticeship Books (see *IR 1* above).

IR 18 Tithe Files. See under *IR 29–30*, below.

IR 19 Specimens of Death Duty Accounts, 1796–1903. Closed for 100 years.

IR 20–5, IR 8 Records of the Land Tax Redemption Office, 1798–1963. These records do *not* relate to lands in Ireland, but individual Irish owners of land in England, Wales and Scotland will appear.

IR 26 Estate Duty Office, Death Duty Registers, 1796–1903. Closed for 100 years. Indexes are in *IR 27*. (NOTE: These records are seen at the PRO, Chancery Lane).

IR 28 Postage Stamps, Correspondence and Papers, 1843–1910. Piece 29 relates to the authorisation of date marks for the districts of distributors of stamps and towns in Ireland, in 1859, and includes twenty-eight specimen date marks. Some other pieces deal with the appointment of distributors of stamps.

IR 29–30, IR 18 Records of the Tithe Commission. The surveys of the commission, appointed under the Tithe Act, 1836, to commute tithe payments into tithe rent charges, covered three-quarters of all the parishes of England and Wales between 1836 and about 1850. They were extremely detailed, and the apportionments in *IR 29* accompanied by very large-scale maps in *IR 30* give information about occupants and land-use, as well as ownership, of each individual plot of land in every parish surveyed. Worth searching for genealogical and other purposes involving individual Irish residents in England and Wales. A leaflet explaining the tithe records in greater detail is available from the PRO.

IR 31 Minutes of the Board of Inland Revenue, Board of Stamps and Board of Stamps and Taxes, 1799–1851. See also *IR 66–7*.

IR 33–9 Records of the War Damage Commission, 1941–73. The War Damage Commission operated under the War Damage Acts, 1941 and 1943, until it was dissolved under the War Damage Act, 1964, when most of its functions were transferred to the Commissioners of Inland Revenue. Broadly, it was responsible for all aspects of assessing and paying compensation for damage caused during and as a result of the Second World War. Its regional offices included one in Belfast. *IR 37/529–38* are regional files relating to specific properties in Belfast. See also *LT 1–2*, below.

IR 40 Stamps and Taxes Division, Registered Files, from 1808. They are concerned with the general oversight of taxation and taxation policy. Specifically Irish affairs crop up from time to time; *IR 40/11*, for example, deals with Irish pawnbrokers' licenses, 1842–3, *IR 40/44* with a vacancy for a stamper in Dublin in 1844, *IR 40/528* with the Land Improvement (Ireland) Bill in 1860.

IR 41 Corporation Duty Files, 1885–1960.

IR 43 Board of Stamps Letter Books (M series), 1807–19. A class of entry books including out-letters from the Board of Stamps to the Irish Board of Stamps. Letters to the Irish Board of Stamps between 1819 and 1827 are entered in *IR 45*. After 1827, when the Irish Board was consolidated with the English, letters dealing with Irish stamp duties are to be found in *IR 47*, a special class of Irish letter books dated October 1827 to December 1833.

IR 49 Board of Stamps, Treasury Letter Books, 1800–33.

IR 50 Board of Stamps, Reports to the Treasury of Legacy Duty Cases, 1825–33.

IR 52 Board of Taxes, Income and Property Tax: Surveyors' Property Letter Books, 1803–16. Entry books of letters and circulars from the Board of Taxes to inspectors and surveyors of taxes following the reimposition in 1803 of a tax on profits arising from property, professions, trades and offices. This tax was repealed in 1816.

IR 53 Board of Taxes, Income and Property Tax: Property Letter Books, 1803–7.

IR 54 Board of Taxes Precedent Books: Assessed Taxes and Inhabited House Duties, 1804–33.

IR 55 Lottery Office Papers, 1713–1833. Papers reflecting the government regulation of both state and private lotteries, including those held in Ireland. *IR 55/30* is a guard book containing amongst other things a collection of tickets in Irish state lotteries, 1796–9. See also the lottery books, in *IR 4*, above.

IR 56 Correspondence relating to Stamp Duty on Newspapers, 1836–70. Includes a few pieces specifically relating to Ireland, e.g. *IR 56/33*, dated 1849–61, on the registration of distinctive dies for certain Irish newspapers and *IR 56/43* on the case of the wrongful arrest of the publisher of the *Dundalk Express*, 1864–7.

IR 60 Board of Taxes Reports to Treasury, 1802–35.

IR 61 Board of Taxes, Treasury Letter Copy Books, 1797–1823. Copies of letters from the Treasury.

IR 63 Budget and Finance Bill Papers, 1869–1950.

IR 64 Statistics and Intelligence Division, Correspondence and Papers, 1858–1965. Includes *IR 64/39*, dated 1918–36, 'Irish Free State: handing over of income tax administration to the Irish. Table of comparison with the UK'.

IR 66 Board of Taxes: Property Tax Precedent Case Books, 1803–21.

IR 67 Board of Taxes: Legacy, Succession and Probate Duty Case Books, 1853–66.

IR 68 Board of Taxes: Assessed Taxes and Inhabited House Duty Precedent Books and Composition Cases, 1819–48.

IR 70 Board of Taxes: Assessed Taxes and Inhabited House Duties, Judges' Opinions, 1805–30.

IR 71 Board of Taxes Miscellaneous Books, 1698–1833. They include annual accounts of returns of establishment, 1778–1833.

IR 72 Board of Stamps Miscellaneous Books, 1694–1857.

IR 73 Board of Inland Revenue Private Office Papers, 1908–18. These mainly relate to budget legislation and to proposals for consideration by the Chancellor of the Exchequer.

IR 74 Private Office Papers: Memoranda, 1700–1967. These relate to a wide range of policy and general matters, including many with implications for taxation in Ireland, although Ireland is not dealt with separately.

IR 75 Private Office Papers: Committee Papers, from 1909. In general, the same remark applies to these as to the memoranda in *IR 74*. There are, however, a few pieces of special relevance to Irish affairs, e.g. *IR 75/52*, 1926–30, Republic of Ireland: conference concerning residents and non-residents for tax purposes; *IR 75/53–5*, Home and Empire statistics, 1920–1; *IR 75/128*, on Northern Ireland re-assessment in 1930 and *IR 75/162–79*, a set of papers relating to the financial and taxation aspects of the Government of Ireland Act, 1921–5.

IR 79 Office of the Director of Stamping, Miscellanea, 1811–1949. *IR 79/175* and *180* relate to stamps, dies and plates in Ireland between 1916 and 1933.

IR 80 Office of the Director of Stamping, Registered Files, 1876–1973. A small amount of specifically Irish material will be found scattered throughout this class, e.g. *IR 80/21*, Irish Free State: new stamping dies, 1923–4; *IR*

80/51, Dublin Offices: burning of the customs house by Irish extremists, etc., 1921–3.

IR 81 Establishment Division Registered Files, 1894–1950. Several files deal with arrangements for tax collection and staffing in Ireland.

IR 83 Miscellanea, 1688–1935. This class emanates from the Board of Stamps, Board of Taxes, Board of Stamps and Taxes, Board of Excise and Board of Inland Revenue. It deals mainly with establishment matters and the legal and policy aspects of taxation.

IR 84 Board of Stamps and Taxes: Miscellaneous Books, 1833–53. They include 'returns of persons in confinement for non-payment of taxes, giving names of prisoners, etc.', 1848–53.

IR 86 Office of Special Commissioners of Income Tax: Miscellaneous Books, 1842–1903. The class relates mainly to the Special Commissioners' responsibilities for hearing appeals against tax assessments and for making various assessments.

IR 98 Office of the Solicitor: Law Officers' and Counsel's Opinions, from 1828. Closed for 100 years

IR 99 Office of the Solicitor: Solicitor's Opinions and Reports, from 1828. Also closed for 100 years.

J: Records of the Supreme Court of Judicature
(NOTE: Kept at the PRO, Chancery Lane)
By the Supreme Court of Judicature Act, 1873 (36 and 37 Vict, c. 66) the then existing courts were consolidated to form one Supreme Court of Judicature in England, consisting of two permanent divisions, a High Court of Justice and a Court of Appeal. The records of the Supreme court, grouped under the Letter J, for the most part continue series from the courts of Chancery, Common Pleas, King's (or Queen's) Bench, etc. They are described in detail in the *Guide to the Contents of the Public Record Office*, vol. 1. While the Supreme Court does not and did not have jurisdiction over any part of Ireland, its records do of course include those of cases and proceedings in England that involved Irish people.

KB: Records of the Court of King's (or Queen's) Bench
(NOTE: Kept at the PRO, Chancery Lane)
These include from 1875 the records of the Crown Office of the King's Bench Division of the High Court of Justice. See above, under *J*, and *Guide to the Contents of the Public Record Office*, vol. 1.

LAB: Records of government departments dealing with labour and employment

LAB records include those of the Labour Department (and its predecessors) in the Board of Trade, whose functions were taken over during the First World War by the newly created Ministry of Labour, subsequently itself replaced by successive departments responsible for labour and employment questions. Although such questions were dealt with mainly at the provincial government level in Ireland, there have always been close connections between Great Britain and Ireland in the sphere of industrial relations, and many trade unions with headquarters in England have had Irish branches. Hence there is a certain amount of material relating to Ireland to be quarried out of *LAB* records. The following are the most useful classes:

LAB 2 Correspondence, 1897–1933 (with a few later papers). This large class contains files on a wide range of business, from general policy to dealings of the department with particular trade boards, individuals, etc., and intervention in particular disputes. The essential finding aid to *LAB 2*, whose arrangement is highly complicated, is the class of indexes, or docket books, in *LAB 7*. A guide to the two classes is available on the reference room shelves at the PRO, Kew, and an expanded descriptive list is being prepared.

The following *LAB* classes also contain scattered references to Irish affairs:

LAB 8 Employment Files, 1909–64.

LAB 9 Finance Files, 1912–73. They include those of bodies related to the Ministry of Labour, such as Remploy and the National Dock Labour Board.

LAB 10 Industrial Relations, General, 1895–1968. Files of the Industrial Relations Department. Until 1934, these overlap with records in *LAB 2*.

LAB 13 Files of the Overseas Department, 1923–61. This class deals mainly with international organisations but also contains papers relating to labour attachés overseas and to the question of labour migration in the United Kingdom. *LAB 13/18* is a Ministry of Labour report on action by Great Britain and Ireland subsequent to recommendations by the International Labour Organisation, 1931–9.

LAB 25 Private Office Papers, 1935–55. Most of this class deals with preparations for and arrangements during the Second World War. Selected post-war case files from the minister's Private Office are in *LAB 42*, but they contain little or nothing on Ireland.

LAB 76 Official Histories: Correspondence and Papers, 1940–53. These unpublished narratives and studies prepared by historians under the supervision of the War Cabinet Committee for Control of Official Histories include *LAB 76/25*, 'Irish Labour in Great Britain, 1939–46' by A.V. Judges (1949). Material from this study was used in the official history by H.M.D. Parker, *Manpower* (HMSO, 1957).

LAR: Land Registry Records.
Although the Land Registration and Land Charges Acts under which the Land Registry functions relate only to England and Wales, *LAR 1*, correspondence and papers, 1822–1967, contains a few references to Ireland, e.g. *LAR 1/234* is a file dated 1928–9 on the Irish Land Purchase Commission.

LCO: Records of the Lord Chancellor's Office

LCO 2 Registered Files, from 1882. These relate to the many functions of the Lord Chancellor, administrative, ecclesiastical, juridical and parliamentary. They include a certain amount relating to Ireland under diverse headings, e.g.: *LCO 2/13*, 1888–9, Lunacy (Ireland), English estates of Irish lunatics; *LCO 2/965*, 1925, Irish peers, procedure in the creation of; *LCO 2/1231*, 1931, proposed settlement of matters outstanding between the Irish Free State and Great Britain, notes of meetings at the Dominions Office; *LCO 2/1441*, 1936, Northern Ireland Great Seal . . .; *LCO 2/1446*, 1923–35, file on Irish representative peers; *LCO 2/1848*, 1937–8, Northern Ireland: consideration as regards UK legislation of the report of a Committee of Inquiry on Trustee Securities; *LCO 2/3919*, 1945, maintenance of married women in desertion cases. Suggested legislation in Northern Ireland to bring the law more into conformity with modern requirements; *LCO 2/4487*, 1949, Ireland Bill.

LR: Exchequer, Records of the Office of the Auditors of Land Revenue (NOTE: Kept at PRO, Chancery Lane)

LR 4 Accounts (Woods), 1663–1831. The class includes records of the land revenues of England and Ireland, 1810–31, described in detail in *Guide to the Contents of the Public Record Office*, vol. I. See also Exchequer records, under *E* above.

LRRO: Records of the Office of Land Revenue Records and Enrolments (For the closely related records of the Crown Estate Commissioners, see above, under *CRES*. Both groups are kept at the PRO, Chancery Lane). Since these records deal with Crown and/or government possessions in both Great Britain and Ireland, with classes going back in some cases to the Tudor period, they are almost all worth searching for material on Ireland. Like the *CRES* records, they are described in detail in *Guide to the Contents of the Public Records Office*, vol. II, and also in the current *Guide* available on the reference room and search room shelves at the PRO, Kew and Chancery Lane. The following classes are particularly likely to be useful to the historian of Ireland:

LRRO 1 Maps and Plans, 1560–1953

LRRO 2 Accounts of the Surveyors General and Commissioners of Woods, 1802–93. (See also *LR 4*, above.)

LRRO 5 Deeds and Evidences, reign of Henry VIII to 1917. Similar to the contents of *CRES 38* (see above).

LRRO 11 Record Agency Papers, 1669–1900. Amongst this collection of correspondence, transcripts of ancient documents, etc., arising out of the record agency work carried out for the Crown by the Keeper of the Land Revenue Records, piece 5 is a pamphlet dated 1870 by H.S. Sweetman, entitled 'Remarks on the Early English Public Records relating to Ireland'.

LRRO 12 Rentals, 1832–1955. Yearly rentals of Crown lands, including those in Ireland.

LRRO 54 Cash Books, 1830–68. They include accounts of the Commissioners of Woods with the Bank of Ireland, 1851–68.

LT: Records of the Lands Tribunal and its predecessors.

The Lands Tribunal, established in 1949 with jurisdiction over the whole United Kingdom except Scotland, took over the duties of arbitrators appointed under earlier Acts, which dealt with covenants affecting land, and related questions of compensation. In 1950 it took over the duties of the War Damage (Valuation Appeals) Panel, which heard appeals against the valuation decisions of the War Damage Commission (for whose records see *IR 33–9*, above).

LT 1 War Damage (Valuation Appeals) Panel, Case Files, 1946–7. Closed to public inspection until 1982, they contain a few Irish cases and are indexed in *LT 2*.

LT 6 General Claims Files, 1939–58. Files on disputes arising out of claims under the Compensation (Defence) Act, 1939, and later Acts dealing with the requisitioning of land and other property. Until 1958 these claims were heard by the General Claims Tribunal, thereafter by the Lands Tribunal. Registers and an index of these claims are in *LT 7*. They include a proportion of Irish cases.

MAF: Records of the Ministry of Agriculture, Fisheries and Food and previous agricultural departments

With the exception of land policy and emergency measures during the Famine, agricultural administration in Ireland has been the business of Irish government bodies more or less since it was recognised as the business of government at all, in either England or Ireland. There is remarkably little material relating to Ireland in *MAF* records, but some scattered references will be found in classes dealing with external relations, with international animal health and disease control and questions of marketing. The following are just a few examples:

MAF 34 Agricultural Marketing Correspondence and Papers, from 1918. *MAF 34/451* consists of papers relating to the Marketing of Fruit Act (Northern Ireland), 1931.

MAF 35 Animal Health Correspondence and Papers, from 1876. *MAF 35/122* deals with import regulations of the Irish Free State on the importation of livestock, 1930–40. *MAF 35/678–83* are later papers on general legislation relating to animal health in Northern Ireland and Eire, but none are yet open under the thirty-year rule.

MAF 40 Trade Relations and International Affairs Correspondence and Papers, from 1839. This class includes papers relating to agricultural policy of the Dominions and Commonwealth and to conferences in which the government of the Irish Republic participated. *MAF 40/180–1* are papers dated 1935–6 on the coal and cattle agreement with Eire.

MEPO: Metropolitan Police records

These records, many of which are subject to extended closure on grounds of sensitivity, are likely to contain references to cases and investigations involving Irish agitators, Fenians, etc. as well as common criminals who happened to be Irish, in London. The lists contain no separate heading for Irish offenders, so that the searcher for Irish material will need to have a good knowledge of particular cases. The following classes are worth noting:

MEPO 1 Office of the Commissioner, Letter Books, 1803–1919.

MEPO 2 Office of the Commissioner, Correspondence and Papers, from 1799.

MEPO 3 Office of the Commissioner, Correspondence and Papers, Supplementary Series, from 1830.

MEPO 4 Office of the Commissioner, Miscellaneous Books and Papers, from 1818. The class includes daily police reports, 1818–38.

MEPO 6 Criminal Record Office, Registers of Habitual Criminals, etc., 1834–1959. Closed for 75 years.

MH: Records of the Ministry of Health and its predecessors including the Poor Law Board and Commission and Local Government Board

MH records cover a wealth of subjects not directly connected with health, as well as almost every aspect of public health administration in Britain. They are particularly rich in sources for the history of 19th-century Poor Law administration; and 20th-century *MH* records constitute an important source of statistical material on public health and other social problems. The class lists reveal almost no specifically Irish material, since administration of the Poor Law, public health, etc. in Ireland was always separate from that in the rest of Britain. But *MH* classes nevertheless are worth searching for information on Poor Law administration in communities (such as Liverpool) where large numbers of Irish people settled.

MH 12 Papers of Poor Law Unions and Other Local Authorities, 1833–1909. Subject indexes to this class appear in *MH 15*, and contain references to the Irish poor in various districts of England.

MH 19 Government Offices, Correspondence and Papers, 1834–1909. These records of the various organs of central government which administered the 19th-century Poor Law include three volumes of correspondence with the Irish Office, 1838–92 (*MH 19/81–3*).

MH 20 Government Offices, Registers of Correspondence, 1838–1920. These registers record correspondence in *MH 19* and in other series which unfortunately no longer exist. *MH 20/43* is a register of correspondence with the Irish Office, 1855–1920.

MH 48 Public Health and Poor Law Services, Local Authority Correspondence, Series I, 1868–1935. Arranged under the names of local authorities, with separate sections for joint hospital boards, asylum boards and port sanitary authorities. A small amount of Irish material may be expected to turn up especially under the latter heading.

MH 52 Public Health and Poor Law Services, Local Authority Correspondence, Series II, from 1913. Also arranged under the names of local authorities.

MH 62 National Health Insurance Administration, Series II, 1912–62. Correspondence of the National Health Insurance Commission for England and the Secretariat of the Joint Committee of the four National Health Insurance Commissions. This includes correspondence with the Irish Commission.

MH 77 Ministry of Health, National Health Service, Post-War Planning and National Health Service Act, 1946. These files include a national survey of hospitals and reports of discussions with numerous professional and other bodies, together with correspondence and surveys of opinion. *MH 77/159* is entitled 'Proposals for a comprehensive health service for the people of Northern Ireland, July – September 1947'.

MINT: Records of the Royal Mint

From 1553 onwards, except briefly during the Civil War and again during the recoinage of the 1690s, the Royal Mint in London was the only one serving England, Wales and Ireland (and Scotland from 1710). *MINT* records are therefore likely to contain references to Ireland and Irish coinage throughout. The following classes are those containing a significant proportion of relevance to Ireland:

MINT 6 Accounts (General), 1677–1907. Ledgers in this class include some accounts with the Bank of Ireland and others relating to Irish coinage, 1824–34 (piece 51).

MINT 7 Coinage: Imperial (General), 1603–1947. Records relating to accounts, contracts, decimal coinage, design of currency, etc. They include some proclamations dealing with Irish coinage and a small amount of correspondence with or relating to offices in Ireland.

MINT 8 Coinage: Imperial (Copper, Bronze and Base Metal), 1672–1943. This class also contains a certain amount of correspondence, accounts, etc. relating to Irish currency.

MINT 9 Coinage: Imperial (Gold and Silver), 1625–1945. Various accounts in this class deal with the Bank of Ireland, and there is some correspondence relevant to Ireland, e.g. *MINT 9/242*, letters and papers dated 1871 on the withdrawal and replacement of worn silver coin circulating in Scotland and Ireland.

MINT 12 Coinage: Channel Islands, Ireland, Isle of Man and Scotland, 1661–1940. Assimilation of the currencies of Great Britain and Ireland was formally proclaimed in December 1825, and most of the papers relating to Ireland in this class deal with the period 1806–25, during which the Mint melted down and minted Spanish dollars (formerly legal currency in Ireland) into Irish silver coins on behalf of the Bank of Ireland and (1822–5) also coined copper half pence and farthings for Ireland. One piece (*MINT 12/22*) deals with the costs of coinage for the Irish Free State, 1928–40, when the Mint was supplying coins of a distinctive design under contract to the Irish Free State. The class list at the PRO, Kew, includes an historical note and cross-references to other classes of *MINT* records.

MINT 13 Coinage: Colonial and Foreign, 1684–1943. This class deals with coinage undertaken by the Mint for foreign and colonial governments, with a few papers relating to International Monetary Conferences, 1867–94. A small amount of Irish business is likely to be traceable in correspondence in this class dealing with coinage in the British Empire and Dominions generally. *MINT 13/237*, dated 1848, is a return of specie supplied for the service of the Commissariat Chests Abroad and to Ireland between 1838 and 1847.

MINT 14 Dies, Matrices and Puncheons, 1685–1943. Papers relating to dies, etc. used by the Mint in coinage for all parts of the world.

MINT 15 Prosecutions for Coinage Offences, 1686–1884. This class may contain papers relating to Irish offenders.

MINT 16 Medals, 1805–48. *MINT 16/40* consists of correpondence dated 1900–1 on a medal issued to commemorate Queen Victoria's visit to Dublin in April 1900.

MINT 19 Newton Papers, reign of William III to 1726. Papers of Sir Isaac Newton as Warden and then master of the Mint. These include a certain amount of Irish material, mainly on coinage but also including a copy of an intended report from the Council of Trade in 1673, on statistics of land, housing, cattle, total wealth, coin and population of Ireland, and another document giving quarterly statistics of Irish customs and excise duties, 1682–8. *MINT 19/6* is a detailed and indexed calendar of the contents of the class.

MINT 20 Registered Files, Annual Series, 1901–67. The subject index which prefaces the class list of *MINT 20* shows a scattering of Irish business of different dates, arranged under various administrative subject headings.

MINT 21 Registers of Correspondence, 1816–1900

MINT 24 Designs of Coins, Medals, Seals, etc., 1926–45. The class includes seals for Northern Ireland, 1933 and 1936, and one for the Irish Free State, 1934.

MT: Records of the Ministry of Transport and other transport departments, including the Marine and Harbour Departments of the Board of Trade
Records in the *MT* group relate to transport of almost every variety by land and water. They deal with roads, railways, waterways, docks, ports, harbours and the high seas. Most *MT* classes will be found to contain some reference to transport in Ireland or around her coasts.

MT 2 Admiralty and Board of Trade Harbour Departments, Out-Letters, 1848–1919. Volumes for 1864–8 contain their own indexes and there are indexes for 1913–18 in *MT 3*. There is a small proportion of references to Ireland in this class, but except for the periods indexed they are difficult to find, as the class list gives only dates and registration numbers of letters.

MT 3 Board of Trade Harbour Departments, Indexes to Out-Letters, 1913–18. Indexes to *MT 2*

MT 4 Marine Out-Letters, 1851–1939. Arranged in a general series and under various subject headings. Indexes are in *MT 5*.

MT 5 Marine Indexes to Out-Letters and Registers of Correspondence, 1864–1918. Indexes to *MT 4*.

MT 6 Railways Correspondence, 1840–1966. These papers relate to the peacetime regulation and wartime control of railways, to railway-owned canals, tramways, etc. and to the central direction of wartime transport. They include material on particular Irish railways and canals, and on the control of Irish railways during and after the First World War. Registers and indexes to this class are in *MT 7* and related out-letters in *MT 11*.

MT 7 Registers and Indexes of Correspondence in *MT 6*, 1840–1919.

MT 9 Marine Correspondence and Papers, 1854–1969. These records relate to various aspects of merchant shipping and navigation in peace and war, and to wrecks and foreshores. They include papers on the administration of marine departments and services in Ireland. Some modern indexes are available in *MT 86* and registers in *MT 85*.

MT 10 Board of Trade Harbour Department Correspondence and Papers, 1864–1920. The class includes material on a variety of different questions affecting Irish harbours, etc. It also includes papers on electricity and gas undertakings. Subject indexes to papers for dates between 1856 and 1885 are in *BT 19*.

MT 11 Board of Trade Railway Department Out-Letters, 1840–55. Entry books of out-letters of the Railway Department and, from 1846 to 1851, the Railway Commissioners. Drafts of out-letters after 1855 are to be found in *MT 6*. The volumes in *MT 11* all contain their own indexes.

MT 12 Board of Trade Railway Department Indexes to Out-Letters, 1855–1917. The letters to which these refer have not survived, but some drafts will be found in *MT 6*.

MT 13 Board of Trade Railway Department Minute Books, 1844–57. The keeping of minute books was discontinued in 1857.

MT 15 Consultative Marine Correspondence and Papers, 1867–1964. These deal with the inspection and survey of ships, engines, boilers, wireless, etc. for safety purposes. Technical information similar to that in this class will also be found in *MT 9* for dates up to 1922.

MT 19 Admiralty Harbour Department, Correspondence and Papers, 1842–65. The class includes a certain amount on improvements and other works in Irish harbours.

MT 20 Board of Trade Marine Department Minute Book, 1857. One volume of minutes of formal meetings of the board, including a little Irish business. The keeping of minutes was discontinued in February 1857.

MT 27 London to Shrewsbury and Holyhead Roads, 1772–1951. Reports of the committees and select committees appointed to enquire into the state of these roads, with reports, accounts, journals of work carried out, correspondence and papers of the Holyhead Road Commissioners appointed in 1815. These committees, etc. resulted from Parliament's concern with the poor state of road communication between England and Ireland. The papers include reports, surveys and designs by Thomas Telford, and accounts and correspondence relating to the upkeep of the roads. Although most of the material deals with the English and Welsh side of the Irish Channel, there is some relating to the administration of Howth harbour.

MT 29 Railway Inspectorate, Inspectors' Reports, 1840–1949. Reports of the inspecting officers of railways, appointed under the Regulation of Railways

Act, 1840. Each volume has its own index, and additional indexes to locations from 1871 are to be found in *MT 30*.

MT 32 Admiralty Transport Department: Surgeon Superintendents' Journals of Convict Ships, 1858–67. Of potential relevance to the later history of the transportation of Irish convicts.

MT 38 Road Board Correspondence and Papers, 1909–28. This class includes papers on the administration of the Road Fund in Ireland, the Irish Advisory Engineering Committee, 1913–20, the road improvement programme for Ireland, 1918, and a minute book of the Irish Advisory Joint Road Committee, 1919.

MT 39 Ministry of Transport, Highways Correspondence and Papers, 1862–1967. Includes papers on Irish roads.

MT 41 Ferries Committee (1941) Correspondence and Papers, 1939–54. The class includes a report on the Island of Lismore ferry and mail service, 1946 and 1947, and some general papers which may include dealings with local authorities in Northern Ireland.

MT 42 Royal Commission on Transport Papers, 1928–31. The commission's brief extended to the whole UK including Northern Ireland.

MT 43 Transport Advisory Council Minutes and Papers, 1934–44.

MT 45 Ministry of Transport, Establishment and Organisation Correspondence and Papers, 1906–69. The class includes files on staff in Ireland and on the transfer of functions under the Ministry of Transport Act, 1919, the Government of Ireland Act, 1920, and the Irish Free State (Agreement) Act, 1922.

MT 47 Ministry of Transport, Finance Correspondence and Papers, 1910–58. The class includes papers on the Irish mail service, Irish railways, unemployment in Ireland and the transfer of powers to the governments of Northern Ireland and the Irish Free State.

MT 49 Geddes Papers, 1919–22. The private office papers of Sir Eric Geddes, the first Minister of Transport, 1919–21. These include papers on Irish railways, roads and mails.

MT 52 Inland Waterways Correspondence and Papers, 1917–64. *MT 52/133* includes a paper on post-war planning for the recruitment of Irish labour, dated 1943–4.

MT 59 Shipping Control and Operation, Correspondence and Papers, 1938–66. Papers dealing with the emergency control of shipping during the Second World War. Amongst a scattering of file titles likely to include material of relevance to Ireland these appear: Northern Ireland trade review, 1938, and particulars of some UK ports (Northern Ireland) (both in *MT*

59/1224); enemy ships detained in Eire, 1940 (*MT 59/2562*); and Eire: request for British shipping assistance: meetings between Eire and UK government representatives, 1939–43 (*MT 59/2585–90*, with related papers in *MT 59/208*).

MT 63 Port and Transit Correspondence and Papers, 1915–57. The class consists mainly of papers on the Ministry of War Transport's control of British and Allied merchant shipping and cargoes in UK and overseas ports during the Second World War. These include (*MT 63/116*) papers of the later Services Security Board on traffic with Eire, 1940–5, and various more general files which are likely to relate partly to Ireland.

MT 85–6 Registers and Indexes of Board of Trade Marine Departments Correspondence in *MT 9* (see above).

MT 91 Board of Trade Railway Department, Drawings and Plans, 1840–*c*.1866. Some plans in this class relate to Irish railways.

MT 101 Marine Branch Establishment Division Files, from 1942. These files of the Ministry of War Transport and, from 1946, the Ministry of Transport, relate to the lighthouse service and include many dealing with the Irish lights service, 1943–51.

MUN: Records of the Ministry of Munitions in the First World War

The arrangement of the records of the Ministry of Munitions is particularly confusing. This is due partly to the ministry's unprecedentedly rapid growth and its frequent reorganisation, and partly to the fact that when the ministry was dissolved after the war its records were left to be arranged by organisations with no working knowledge of it. Furthermore, many important papers were extracts and rearranged for the benefit of official historians. There is a card index to the records of the Historical Records Branch (*MUN 5*) in the reference room at the PRO, Kew, and an index to the Central Registry records (*MUN 4*) is in course of preparation. A copy of the official *History of the Ministry of Munitions* is also available at Kew, and has been published on microfiche by Harvester Press, Brighton. It contains a section on the ministry's area organisation in Ireland (vol. II, section II, chap. XIV). Some of the records on which this history is based survive in *MUN 5* and refer to such subjects as the organisation of munitions work in Ireland, cross-channel traffic between England and Ireland, the post-war utilisation of national factories in Ireland, importation of Irish labour for munitions work in England and the position of Irish labour with regard to the Military Service Act. There are almost certainly related records in *MUN 4*. Apart from these two classes, however, only a small proportion of the records created by the ministry has survived. The papers of David Lloyd George as Minister of Munitions (1915–16) are in *MUN 9*. They do not appear from the class list to contain anything of direct relevance to Ireland, although they do contain much on general policy.

MUN 4 Records of the Central Registry, etc., 1909–37. Documents not only of the Ministry of Munitions but also of the Disposal and Liquidation Commission and of the Surplus Stores etc. Liquidation Departments of the Treasury.

MUN 5 Historical Records Branch Records, 1901–43. (See above).

NATS: Records of the Ministry of National Service in the First World War

NATS 1 Ministry of National Service Records, 1916–20. The ministry was established in 1917 to deal with recruitment both to the armed forces and to civil labour. This, the only class of its records, contains both policy and administrative files on a wide range of subjects relating to recruitment. *NATS 1/245–67* are files of the Irish National Recruiting Council, 1917–20; *NATS 1/1041* deals with the position of Irishmen under United States conscription laws in 1918; and *NATS 1/1140* is a file on the employment of Irishmen on munitions work. Some other files in the class will probably be found to contain material relevant to Irish Labour.

NDO: Records of the National Debt Office

The National Debt Office was in existence continuously from 1786, when commissioners were appointed under the National Debt Reduction Act, until April 1980, when it merged with the Public Works Loan Board (for whose records see *PWLB*, below) to form the National Investment and Loans Office. From 1816, when the separate commissioners for Ireland were abolished, English and Irish business was conducted together. The various *NDO* classes of records reflect the wide variety of schemes administered by the National Debt Office, and several (e.g. *NDO 1–2*, life annuities and tontine, 1745–89) are likely to record dealings with individual Irish people. The following classes specifically include Irish business:

NDO 3 Irish Tontines, 1773–7. Records dated 1773–1871. The last survivor of the three Irish tontines of the 1770s died in 1870. These records include the registers of subscribers and nominees, payments books, certificates of deaths and marriages, correspondence, etc.

NDO 5 Rules of Closed Savings Banks, from *c*.1817. The class includes banks in Ireland.

NDO 7 National Debt Office Correspondence, 1808–1942. Each volume is indexed and piece *NDO 7/45* is a complete index to the class. Irish correspondence will be found scattered throughout. *NDO 7/46* and *47* deal specifically with the Irish Church Temporalities Commission, 1870–81; and *NDO 7/48* is miscellaneous papers on the Irish Land Commision, Irish Church, etc., 1881–93.

NDO 11–12 Trustee Savings Bank Inspection Committee Minutes, from 1891.

NDO 13 Registered Files, from 1894. Irish affairs occur in several parts of this class. For example, *NDO 13/1* contains accounts of the Benefit Branch of the Royal Irish Constabulary Force Fund, 1928–56 (and will therefore not be open until 1987, thirty years after the latest date on the file); *NDO 13/77–94* is a series of accounts connected with Irish land purchase, the majority of which also extend into the 1950s and therefore are not yet open to public inspection.

NDO 15 Comptroller–General's Out-Letters, 1873–1938. They contain a quantity of material on Irish affairs, especially Irish land purchase, and include indexes.

NDO 16 Trustee Savings Bank Inspection Committee, Annual Reports, from 1892.

NDO 17 Trustee Savings Bank Year Books, from 1934.

NIA: *Records of the National Insurance Audit Department*
This department was set up in 1912 to audit the accounts of the approved societies (insurance companies, friendly societies and trade unions) which administered National Health Insurance under the National Insurance Act, 1911. In 1948 the approved societies were dissolved under the National Health Service Act, 1946, and the work of the department came to an end.

NIA 3 Specimens of Documents Destroyed, 1912–43. This class includes copies of auditors' reports on approved societies and insurance committees in Cork, Longford, West Meath and Wicklow. Annual reports of the department are in *NIA 2*

NSC: *Records of the Department for National Savings and of the National Savings Committee for England and Wales.*
The records of this group almost all relate only to England and Wales (although the usual warning applies, that the affairs of individual Irish residents in England and Wales, can, of course, crop up anywhere).

NSC 11 Savings Certificate Office Correspondence and Papers, 1915–51. The class contains papers on the sale and repayment of savings certificates in the Commonwealth, with one file (*NSC 11/254*) on both Southern and Northern Ireland in 1921. Another file, *NSC 11/314*, is entitled 'Procedure: mental incapacity: Irish republic, 1940' and very possibly other examples dealing with Irish subject matter could be found.

OS: *Records of the Ordnance Survey Department*

OS 1 Ordnance Survey Correspondence and Papers, 1791–1974. This class includes material on survey work in Ireland and other administrative material dealing with Ireland.

OS 5 Maps and Plans, 1777–1962. *OS 5/35* is a plan of Mountjoy Barracks, *c.* 1900.

OS 6 Papers on Magnetic Surveys of Great Britain, 1914–33. The class includes descriptions of magnetic survey stations in Ireland, 1914–15, computation books, 1914–15, which include Ireland, and calculation books, 1924–5, including Ireland.

PC: Records of the Privy Council
(NOTE: Kept at the PRO, Chancery Lane)

PC 1 Unbound Papers, 1481–1946. This very large class reflects the enormously varied work of the Privy Council. It includes: petitions and letters to the Council; reports and memorials from government departments and committees of the Council, law officers' opinions; papers in appeal cases; orders and minutes of the Council, proclamations, precedents, etc. Subject matter includes Irish parliamentary bills, but much more undoubtedly can be unearthed relating to Ireland. Amongst other potential sources of Irish material within the class is a collection of papers of the Prince de Bouillon (for whose significance and other papers see *FO 95* and *HO 69*, above, and *WO 1*, below) and of the Comte de Calonne, *Contrôleur de France* 1783–7, whose links with British spies, French emigrés, etc. also involved him in Irish affairs. Detailed lists, keys and other finding aids to *PC 1* are available at the PRO, Chancery Lane, and many of the colonial papers for the period 1676–1983 are calendared in *Acts of the Privy Council of England, Colonial Series*, vol. VI (1912).

PC 2 Privy Council Registers, 1540–1920. They contain minutes of the Council's proceedings, certain proclamations and the reports of committees with the papers accompanying them. The volumes are fully indexed. Other records of the Privy Council which are worth searching for material relating to Ireland include:

PC 4 Minutes, 1670–1928.

PC 6 Miscellaneous Books, 1660–1900. The class includes some minutes of the Commissioners and Committee for Ireland for various dates between 1671 and 1691.

PC 7 Letter Books, 1825–99.

PC 8 Original Correspondence, 1860–1949.

PC 9 Registers of Correspondence, 1860–1949.

PC 12 Supplementary Original Correspondence, 1898–1949.

PCOM: Records of the Prison Commission and its predecessors.

PCOM 1 Old Bailey Sessions Papers, 1801–1904 (see also *CRIM 1* and *HO 16*, above). Printed proceedings of the Commissions of Oyer and Terminer and Gaol Delivery for the areas within the jurisdiction of the Central Criminal Court (Old Bailey). Each volume is indexed.

PCOM 2 Prison Records, Series I, 1770–1916. Registers of prisoners and habitual criminals, photograph albums, minute books, etc. relating to prisons in England and Wales, to Gibraltar prison and to some ship prisons. Closed for 100 years. Other records in the *PCOM* group which are well worth searching for individual Irish prisoners are in:

PCOM 3–4 Male and Female Licences, 1853–87. These are notes of licences to convicts to be at large and in some cases include transfer papers which otherwise are to be found in *PCOM 5*. Registers are in *PCOM 6*.

PCOM 5 Old Captions and Transfer papers, 1843–71. 'Old captions' were court orders for the imprisonment or transportation of convicts. Transfer papers authorised the removal of a convict to a government prison, and in both cases the penal records and other particulars of the prisoners were included. Registers are in *PCOM 6*.

PCOM 6 Registers and Indexes, 1824–85. These refer to *PCOM 3–5*, above. They are closed for 100 years.

PCOM 7 Registered Papers, Series I, 1838–1938. Registered files dealing with the management of prisons and treatment of prisoners. Most of these papers span the period 1877–1929, when a new registration system was introduced. Since they deal with general matters of prison administration and policy, these papers are likely only to be of tangential use of Irish historians, e.g. in providing evidence of the sort of conditions endured by prisoners in Britain at various times.

PCOM 8 Registered Papers, Supplementary Series I, 1876–1941. These are closed for 75 or 100 years, and relate mainly to particular criminals.

PIN: Records of the Ministry of Pensions and National Insurance, together with those of other departments dealing with national insurance, pensions and unemployment insurance.

PIN 2 National Health Insurance Commissions and Joint Committtee, 1911–45. The class includes minutes of the Joint Committee, 1911–48, on which Ireland (after 1922 Northern Ireland) was represented.

PIN 4 Pensions and Insurance, 1911–58. Some files deal with Northern Ireland regulations and reciprocal arrangements with the Irish Free State. See also *PIN 34*.

PIN 7 Labour Exchanges and Unemployment, from 1911. Files relating to the general and financial administration of labour exchanges and unemployment insurance, including a few of relevance to Ireland, e.g. *PIN 7/41* 'Ireland – extension to various trades, 1919'; *PIN 7/62* and *129* 'Reciprocal arrangements between Great Britain, the Irish Free State and Northern Ireland, 1922 and 1932–3'. See also *PIN 34.*

PIN 12 Workmen's Compensation Correspondence, 1900–56. Includes *PIN 12/73*, dated 1934–41, on the jurisdiction of courts in Northern Ireland under the Workmen's Compensation Act.

PIN 15 War Pensions Correspondence and Papers, from 1901. This class includes papers of the British War Pensions Advisory Committee which oversees the payment and administration of war pensions to people living outside the UK, including people in Eire. Various other papers in the class relate to Irish matters, e.g. to the Criminal Injuries (Ireland) Act, 1919, and the Eire Children's Allowance Act, 1944, and to the administration of medical benefits in Northern Ireland.

PIN 18 Registered Files, F Series, 1942–72. These files relate to financial arrangements for national insurance, family allowances, war pensions, unemployment insurance, etc. Some of them deal with reciprocal arrangements with Eire. See also *PIN 34.*

PIN 21 Registered Files: I Series (Industrial Injuries), from 1941. Some files in this class refer to reciprocal arrangements with Northern Ireland for the administration and payment of compensation and insurance connected with industrial injuries. See also *PIN 32* and *34.*

PIN 32 Registered Files: H Series, 1935–66. A selection of files relating to some of the problems arising out of the implementation of the National Insurance Act, 1946, and the National Insurance (Industrial Injuries) Act, 1946. *PIN 32/26*, dated 1947, refers to reciprocal arrangements with Northern Ireland for increased contributory pensions. See also *PIN 34.*

PIN 34 International Relations Division: Reciprocal Arrangements, 1945–71. Several files in this class relate to Northern Ireland and Eire. Since almost the whole class, however, consists of files ending in 1950 or later, relatively little is yet open to public inspection under the thirty-year rule.

PIN 40 Selected War Pensions Appeals, 1944–71. Piece 2 consists of appeals in Scotland and Northern Ireland, where individuals could appeal to a Pensions Appeal Tribunal and thence to a judge of the Supreme Court, against decisions of the Minister of Pensions on entitlement to war pensions.

PMG: Records of the Paymaster General's Office
They include a large number of classes dealing with the British civil, military and naval establishments and with payments to personnel in more specific

categories (e.g. *PMG 23*, coastguards). Most, if not all *PMG* classes would be worth searching for references to Irish individuals. Note especially:

PMG 23 Coastguard Civil Pensions, 1855–1935.

PMG 48 Royal Irish Constabulary Pensions, etc., 1873–1925. This class relates to pensions and allowances made to personnel of the RIC and their widows and children. It includes registers of deceased pensioners, 1877–1918, and rolls of awards of pensions made on the disbandment of the force in 1922.

PMG 74 Correspondence and Papers, from 1730. These general files of the Paymaster General's Office include a number relating specifically to various aspects of the office's administration in Ireland.

POST: *Records of the Post Office.*
Under the terms of the Public Records Act, 1958, they are kept at the Post Office Headquarters Building, St. Martin le Grand, London EC 1.

POWE: *Records of the Ministry of Power and its predecessors.*

POWE 2 Board of Trade, Industrial Power and Transport Department, Water Power Resources Committee, 1906–25. The papers include: *POWE 2/29*, a memorandum dated 1919 on the functions, duties and power of the Commissioners of Public Works, Ireland; and *POWE 2/44*, a paper of 1919 urging the claims of the Irish sub-committee for more funds. Other scattered references to Irish water power will be found in this class.

POWE 10 Establishment Division Correspondence and Papers, from 1887. These include a few files on personnel and related matters dealing with Northern Ireland.

POWE 16 Coal Division, Early Correspondence and Papers, 1896–1953. Some files relate to various aspects of the coal supply in Ireland. (*POWE 16/504*, for example, dated 1919, contains papers on an investigation into the Irish coal mining industry).

POWE 17 Coal Division, Correspondence and Papers on Emergency Services, 1937–58. These papers deal with the supply and regulation of coal, coke, anthracite, etc. during the Second World War and up to the end of rationing in 1956. A few pieces deal with supply in Northern Ireland.

POWE 18 Coal Division, Fuel and Lighting Correspondence and Papers, 1939–58. The class includes a little on Northern Ireland, although it should be noted that most files extend well into the 1950s and so will remain closed for some time under the thirty-year rule.

POWE 26 'A' files, from 1902. They relate to a wide variety of subjects, including various emergency arrangements, mineral transport, metalliferous mining, war-time controls of the mining industry, etc. Here too Irish affairs crop up from time to time: for example *POWE 26/39* contains observations on the Irish coal industry and the application to Ireland of the Mining Industry Act, 1920 (1920–1).

POWE 29 Gas Division Correspondence and Papers, 1877–1961. Amongst scattered material of Irish relevance in this class, most of which will be found in files of more general application, is one dated 1940–6 on the authorisation under Defence Regulation 56 for the Minister of Commerce to act in respect of all gas undertakings in Northern Ireland.

POWE 33 Petroleum Division Correspondence and Papers, 1916–67. This class covers all matters relating to government intervention and legislation affecting the supply and distribution of oil, petroleum and associated products. It includes material on research projects. *POWE 33/17–19* consists of files on civil vulnerable points, petrol storage depots in the UK and Northern Ireland, 1931 and 1934. Various other files will undoubtedly be found to contain material of relevance to Ireland.

PREM: Records of the Prime Minister's Office
The main classes in this group are: *PREM 1*, correspondence and papers, 1916–40; *PREM 3*, operations papers, 1938–46, supplemented by the confidential papers, 1939–46, in *PREM 4*; *PREM 8*, correspondence and papers, 1945–51; and *PREM 11*, correspondence and papers, 1951–64. Some papers in each class are closed for longer than thirty years. The collection as a whole deals with the central direction of government policy by the Prime Minister and contains, therefore, a considerable amount of policy in and towards Ireland, especially for periods when Irish affairs loomed large in British politics and administration. Each of these classes is arranged under subjects, with separate headings for Ireland (or Eire) in *PREM 1, 3–4*. Other *PREM* classes include *PREM 2*, honours lists and papers, 1915–41, including *PREM 2/25* on honours given on the opening of the Ulster Parliament in 1921; *PREM 5*, appointments papers, from 1907, dealing with the ministerial, civil and ecclesiastical appointments for which the Prime Minister is directly responsible; and *PREM 7*, private collections, 1939–51, consisting of the papers of Sir Desmond Morton, who was personal assistant to the Prime Minister from 1940 to 1945.

PRO: Records and papers of the Public Record Office itself, including gifts, deposits or purchases of private papers and transcripts of records in other repositories.

PRO 30 This collection comprises over ninety sub-classes of records given to or deposited with the Public Record Office by private individuals or institutions and in a few cases bought by the Office. In many cases these are the papers of prime ministers and other ministers of the Crown, high-ranking military personnel, leading civil servants and other notable public figures, often including documents relating to their families over several generations.

Taken together, the collection is vast and unclassifiable. Among the more important sources for Irish history within it are:

PRO 30/32 Allan Papers, reign of Queen Victoria. They consist mainly of papers on ecclesiastical history collected by Major-General Alexander S. Allan, and include a considerable amount on Ireland which, although collected in the 19th century, covers many previous centuries.

PRO 30/5 Carew Papers, *c.*1528–1641. Although they are of an earlier date than most of the records mentioned in this guide, it may be helpful to note that they include a MS Chronicle of Ireland, 1589–1616, proceedings of the Irish Parliament, 1613–15, an entry book of Sir Francis Walsingham's letters to Ireland, 1578–9, and his diary for 1570–83.

PRO 30/6 Carnarvon Papers, 1833–98. Mainly the private and official papers of the fourth Earl of Carnarvon who was Secretary of State for the Colonies 1866–7 and 1874–8, as well as holding other ministerial posts. Lord Carnarvon was also Lord Lieutenant of Ireland, 1885–6, and the papers on Ireland, which are indexed, relate mainly to this period. Another collection of Carnarvon papers is in the British Library.

PRO 30/8 Chatham Papers, reigns of George II and George III. Correspondence of the two Prime Ministers, William Pitt, first Earl of Chatham and his son William Pitt the younger, including personal and family correspondence. The class list at the PRO, Kew, contains a subject list and an index to principal correspondents. *PRO 30/8/320–31* contain a quantity of correspondence on Ireland with Pitt the younger between about 1785 and 1798, and there is a scattering of other Irish material in the class. See also *PRO 30/58* and *30/70*, below.

PRO 30/9 Colchester Papers, 1613–19. They include the papers of Charles Abbot, first Lord Colchester, as Chief Secretary for Ireland in 1801, with some later correspondence of Abbot relating to Ireland. *The Diary and Correspondence of Charles Abbot . . . ,* ed. Charles, second Lord Colchester, (London, 1861) was compiled from the journal with interpolated correspondence for 1757–1829 which makes up pieces 31–7 in this class.

PRO 30/11 Cornwallis Papers, 1612–1854. Mainly official papers of the first Marquis Cornwallis relating to the American War of Independence and to Indian civil and military administration. *PRO 30/11/263* contains a mixture of papers on Ireland, dated 1756, 1774 and 1798. The Cornwallis papers are described and indexed in detail in the class list at the PRO, Kew.

PRO 30/22 Russell Papers, *c.*1800–1913. These consist mainly of the private and semi-official papers of the Prime Minister Lord John Russell, later Earl Russell. They are very fully indexed and described in the class lists at the PRO, Kew, and contain a large quantity of material relating to Ireland under a wide range of headings.

PRO 30/24 Shaftesbury papers, reign of Henry II, to 1866. (NOTE: Kept at the PRO, Chancery Lane). Although this collection includes letters and papers of the Ashley and Cooper families in the 18th and 19th centuries, the great bulk of letters and papers relating to Ireland consists of those of the first Earl of Shaftesbury and covers the period roughly 1640–1700.

PRO 30/26 Miscellaneous Gifts and Deposits, 974–1941. Irish material in this class includes: *PRO 30/26/46*, papers of James, first Viscount Limerick (afterwards third Earl of Clanbrassil), *c.*1707–55, with papers of the Cambric Company of Dundalk and others relating to the cambric trade, *c.* 1735–55; and *PRO 30/26/60–4*, a collection of entry books relating to a wide range of civil and military matters in Ireland, some undated, mostly *c.*1715–17.

PRO 30/29 Granville Papers, 1604–1909. The bulk of this large collection consists of private and semi-official papers of the first and second Earls Granville, but there are also some papers of the first earl's father, the second Earl Gower and first Marquis of Stafford and other members of the Granville-Leveson-Gower family. Two separate indexes which form part of the class list at the PRO, Kew, refer to 32 letters and papers of the second Earl Gower and first Marquis of Stafford on the affairs of Ireland between 1774 and 1785, and to a quantity of papers of his son and especially of his grandson (Gladstone's Foreign Secretary) on a wide variety of Irish subjects in the 19th century.

PRO 30/35 Carmichael Smyth Papers, 1805–60. Papers of Major-General Sir James Carmichael Smyth of the Royal Engineers, including *PRO 30/35/15*, a copy of an Ordnance Survey report on Ireland in 1828.

PRO 30/40 Ardagh Papers, 1862–1908. Papers of Major-General Sir John Charles Ardagh (1840–1907), an Anglo-Irish army officer born and educated in Co. Waterford. Ardagh's army career had little to do with Ireland, but the index to his papers (with the class list at the PRO, Kew) shows a few references to Ireland and Irish affairs.

PRO 30/42 Nicholl Papers, 1787–1821. Papers of Sir John Nicholl, who was King's Advocate General from 1798 to 1809. They relate mainly to maritime and international questions referred to him by the Privy Council and the Secretaries of State for Home and Foreign Affairs. Included among them are papers on the prize case of *La Madona*, seized in Ireland in 1801, and on arrangements for dealing with other prize cases in Ireland.

PRO 30/43 Lowry Cole Papers, 1752–1843. The bulk of this collection consists of papers of Sir (Galbraith) Lowry Cole (1772–1842) who served with the 27th Inniskillings in Sicily, 1806–9, commanded the 4th division in the peninsula, 1809–15, and the 1st division at Cambrai, 1815–18, and was Governor of Mauritius, 1823–8, and of Cape Colony, 1828–33. He was also MP for Enniskillen, 1798–1800, and for Fermanagh, 1803–23. The papers include two leases of land in Kinawley, Co. Fermanagh (*PRO 30/43/105/1*) and an account of Sir Lowry Cole's funeral in Ireland in 1842 (*PRO 30/43/117/2*).

PRO 30/47 Egremont Papers, 1672–1769. Papers of Charles, second Earl of

Egremont, Secretary of State for the Southern Department 1761–3. They include papers on the negotiations leading to the peace of Paris, 1763, and on colonial and domestic affairs. *PRO 30/47/24* contains details of dispositons of forces in Ireland and elsewhere in 1762; and *PRO 30/47/27* is a collection of miscellaneous letters on Irish affairs and other matters, 1761–2.

PRO 30/50 Neville and Aldworth Papers, 1476–1834. (NOTE: Kept at the PRO, Chancery Lane) These documents, formerly among the papers of Lord Braybrooke at Audley End, include papers relating to the public careers during the 17th and 18th centuries of several members of the Neville and Aldworth families. They are not rich in Irish material, but *PRO 30/50/12* contains papers relating to the assignment from Richard to John Aldworth of the office of Chief Remembrancer in Ireland, dated 1670, 1677 and 1700.

PRO 30/51 Cairns papers, 1856–85. Papers of Hugh McCalmont, first Earl Cairns (1819–85) including a collection of 'letters of persons associated with Ireland', 1860–85. There is an index of correspondents with the class list.

PRO 30/52 League of Nations Assembly and Council Documents, 1920–46. These consist of: i) records of the London office of the League, ii) official journals of the League, with related indexes and supplementary publications and iii) papers of D.H. Boggis-Rolfe, a member of the League of Nations delegation enquiring into the financial situation in Bulgaria in 1933. The class contains its own indexes and subject indexes, showing references, for example, to the admissions of the Irish Free State to the League in 1923.

PRO 30/57 Kitchener Papers, 1877–38. Papers of the first Earl Kitchener of Khartoum, including a small amount of correspondence relating to Ireland, almost all of which dates from the period of the First Word War. *PRO 30/57/60* consists of correspondence on Ireland in 1914, and other references will be found through the index at the end of the class list.

PRO 30/58 Dacres Adams Papers, 1676–1856. This collection mostly pertains to William Dacres Adams, a clerk in the secretary of state's office, 1791–1810, private secretary to William Pitt the younger during his last ministry, 1804–6, and to the Duke of Portland, 1807–9. It includes some official papers of Pitt and Portland. The class list contains no hint of Irish relevance and the accompanying index is to names of correspondents only. A sample inspection shows, however, that material relating to Ireland is to be found in this class. For example, *PRO 30/58/3*, item no. 65, consists of a letter to Pitt from Lord Buckingham dated 4 September 1800 on Irish law and law courts, with a long unsigned memorandum in another hand on the constitution, representation, etc. of Ireland, including franchise reform and taxation. See also *PRO 30/8*, above, and *PRO 30/70*, below.

PRO 30/59 Sturgis Diary, July 1920–Jan 1922. The diary of Sir Mark Sturgis as joint Assistant Under-Secretary for Ireland.

PRO 30/60 Balfour Papers, 1880–1907. Papers of A.J. Balfour as Chief Secretary for Ireland, 1887–91 and of his brother G.W. Balfour in the same post, 1896–1900, together with those of G.W. Balfour as President of the Board of Trade and President of the Local Government Board, to 1905. The Irish papers are closed to public inspection until they are 100 years told, in conformity with those in *HO 144* (see above).

PRO 30/64 Lt-General Sir Charles Napier's Papers, 1798–1854. They include correspondence between Sir Charles Napier and his life-long friend Lt-Col John Kennedy who was noted for his agricultural experiments settling Irish paupers on the land and for his engineering achievements in Cephalonia and India. Among this correspondence is a set of printed letters relating to the Royal Hospital, Kilmainham, between 1830 and 1835.

PRO 30/66 Mance papers, 1899–1924. Papers of Brigadier-General Sir. H. Osborne Mance relating to his career in the army (1899–1918) and as an internationally recognised communications expert acting as British delegate to the 1919–20 Peace Conference and to various League of Nations conventions on problems of transport in post-war Europe. They include correspondence and papers dated 1914–18 on the shipment of troops to Ireland (*PRO 30/66/9*).

PRO 30/67 Midleton Papers, 1885–1941. Papers of St John Broderick, first Earl of Midleton (1856–1942), who after holding various posts in Conservative governments from 1895–1905, became leader of the Southern Unionists in Ireland. *PRO 30/67/27–57* are devoted to Irish affairs. The class list includes an alphabetical key to correspondents, with notes on the positions they held.

PRO 30/69 Ramsay Macdonald Papers. Official and personal papers of J. Ramsay Macdonald (the first Labour Prime Minster) and his wife and family. Reference to Irish affairs will be found scattered throughout. Files specifically devoted to Ireland among the offical papers deal with Irish immigration to the UK, 1929–35 (*PRO 30/69/358*); memoranda of the Irish situation committee of the Cabinet, 1934 (*PRO 30/69/612*); and de Valera and the Irish situation, 1932 (correspondence and papers) (*PRO 30/69/701*).

PRO 30/70 Hoare Pitt Papers, 1667–1946. They supplement the Chatham papers (*PRO 30/8*) and Dacres Adams papers (*PRO 30/58*) and contain mainly official, semi-official and family correspondence of the first and second Earls of Chatham and of William Pitt the younger. Both the family and the official correspondence includes a scattering of references to Irish affairs. Indexes of correspondents and of place names accompany the class list.

PRO 30/89 Wylie Papers. Papers of William Evelyn Wylie (1881–1964). Son of the Rev. R.D. Wylie of Coleraine, W.E. Wylie held the posts of Law Adviser to the Irish Government, 1919–20, Judge of the Supreme Court of Judicature (Ireland) 1920–4 and Judge of the High Court of the Irish Free State, 1924–36. Among other interests he was Vice-Chairman of the Irish Betting Control Board, a steward of the Irish Turf Club, President of the Royal Dublin Society, Vice-Chairman of the Irish Red Cross Society and a member of the Irish Railways Wages Board. These papers, given to the PRO by his daughter, are predominantly of a personal nature. They include a MS memoir (dated 1939 and 1951) and a few official papers, mainly dating from 1920–4.

PRO 31 Transcripts (NOTE: All kept at Chancery Lane)

PRO 31/1 Carte Papers, 1571–1689. Mainly dealing with the affairs of Ireland between 1640 and 1685, they are transcripts of the official papers collected by Thomas Carte for his *Life of James, Duke of Ormonde*.

PRO 31/3 Paris Archives, Baschet's Transcripts, 1504–1714. Transcripts of documents in the Archives Nationales de France relating to Great Britain and Ireland.

PRO 31/8 Record Commission Transcripts, Series II, n.d. They include four volumes of transcripts of documents formerly in the Irish series of State Papers, which were later deposited in the Library of Philadelphia and then returned to Great Britain, deposited in the Public Record Office of Ireland, and destroyed by fire on 30 June 1922.

PROB: *Records of the Prerogative Court of Canterbury*
(NOTE: Kept at the PRO, Chancery Lane)
This is a large collection of probate records dating in some cases from as early as the 15th century, to the mid 19th century. It has no direct bearing on Ireland, but many of the classes (some of which are still under arrangement) would repay searching for the wills, administrations, etc. of individual Irish people or owners of property in Ireland. A leaflet, describing *PROB* records in some detail is available from the PRO, and PRO Handbook no. 19, *Tracing your Ancesters in the Public Record Office* (London, HMSO, 1981) is now on sale.

PWLB: *Records of the Public Works Loan Commissioners (subsequently Public Works Loan Board)*
The origins of this board lie in an Act of 1817 which authorised payments by Exchequer bills and from the Consolidated Fund for carrying out public works and to employ the poor. Originally there were separate commissioners for England and Ireland, but the records reflect work undertaken in both countries. The modern function of the board, dating from its reconstitution under the Public Works Loans Act, 1875, was to make loans to local authorities and other public bodies for public works, and to harbour authorities, housing associations, companies, societies and even to private persons for the provision of houses. Other loans made by the board included long-term credits to farmers and to the Territorial Army associations. In 1980 the Public Works Loan Board merged with the National Debt Office to form the new National Investment and Loans Office. *PWLB* classes, the earliest of which are in *PWLB 2* (minute books, 1817–1950, indexed) and *PWLB 6* (registers of applications for loans from 1811) contain a scattering of references to public works in Ireland throughout.

RAIL: Records of railway and canal companies, formerly kept by British Rail as the British Transport Historical Records.
This enormous collection of records relating to rail and water transport from the days of the earliest canals mostly predates the implementation of the Transport Act, 1947, which nationalised the railways, road haulage and various other forms of transport in Great Britain. There is, however, some overlap in dates between these classes and those in the *AN* group which contains records of the British Transport Commission and other bodies established under the Act. A card index to the British Transport Historical Records is kept in the reference room at the PRO, Kew, and a brief guide to the records is also available. *RAIL* classes divide roughly into general records, which contain a good deal on Ireland, and records of particular companies. While only *RAIL 131* and *162* deal specifically with Irish companies, there is a considerable amount of material dealing with Ireland among the records of the Great Western Railway Company and the London and North Western Railway Company. The followng classes should be noted in particular:

RAIL 131 Cork City Railway Company, 1906–25.

RAIL 162 Dundalk, Newry and Greenore Railway Company, 1863–1957.

RAIL 206 Fishguard and Rosslare Railways and Harbours Company, 1898–1947.

RAIL 253 Great Western Railway Company, Miscellaneous Books and Records, 1800–61. These include photograph albums showing steamships on the route to Ireland and scenes in Ireland, other records of the steamship service to Ireland, reports and returns on Irish traffic, reports on the visits of directors and other officials of the company to Ireland, and excursion handbills and other ephemera.

RAIL 257 Great Western Railway Company, Correspondence and Papers, 1849–1949. The only piece in this class whose title specifically refers to Ireland is *RAIL 257/5*, letters and papers relating to the Waterford and Central Ireland Railway and the Waterford and Kilkenny Railway, 1866–79.

RAIL 258 Great Western Railway Company Secretarial Papers, 1835–1963. These include annual reports of the Traffic Department which sometimes refer to Irish traffic, and papers on insurance and other financial matters affecting Irish routes.

RAIL 266 Great Western Railway Company, Various Statistics, 1867–1959. *RAIL 266/42* consists of Fishguard harbour traffic statistics, 1927–42.

RAIL 327 Irish and English Traffic Conference, from 1874.

RAIL 410 London and North Western Railway Company Records, 1803–1953. These include records relating to the company's Irish steamboat service, exchanges of information with Irish companies on traffic, and various deeds and agreements concerning vessels, stations, etc. on the Irish cross-channel service.

RAIL 941 Ireland: Air, Rail and Road Timetables, from 1859.

RAIL 1019 Canals, Docks, and Shipping Collection, from 1760. A general collection of prospectuses, maps, plans, etc. which contains a few items relating to water transport in Ireland.

RAIL 1062 Parliamentary: Railway and Canal Acts, *c*.1720–1940. This class and the two following constitute a fairly comprehensive (but not complete) set of Acts of Parliament relating to railways and canals, including several dealing with Ireland.

RAIL 1063 Parliamentary: Special Acts, from 1685.

RAIL 1064 Parliamentary: Supplementary Acts, from 1722.

RAIL 1066 Parliamentary Bills and Minutes of Evidence, etc., 1825–1953. Worth searching for Irish material, this class relates mainly to railways but also includes some papers on canals, docks and tramways.

RAIL 1068 Parliamentary Bills and Minutes of Evidence other than Railways and Canals, 1855–1946. This class includes a wide variety of subjects involving improvements to local amenities, e.g. tramways, docks, bridges, electric lighting, street widening, etc. It is arranged in alphabetical order of place and includes a small amount on Dublin.

RAIL 1071 Parliamentary: Deposited Plans, n.d. The class includes a plan for an extension of North Wall quay, Dublin, in 1872 (*RAIL 1071/135*).

RAIL 1075 Prospectuses: Railways and Other Undertakings, 1819–1950. The class includes a small amount of Irish material.

RAIL 1076 Prospectuses: Railways and Other Undertakings (York Collection), 1818–1943. The class includes one prospectus, *RAIL 1076/11*, for the Cork and Kinsale Junction Railway, 1858.

RAIL 1080–1097 Records of the Railway Clearing House, from 1842. These includes deeds, agreements, etc., junction diagrams, regulations and classification of goods, minutes and reports, miscellaneous books and records, staff records and station handbooks. The considerable amount of Irish material in these classes includes papers on Irish and English Livestock and Traffic Conferences, the Irish Railway Clearing House, and Irish railway managers' meetings.

RAIL 1119 Reports of Commissions, from 1832. Evidence to and reports of Royal and other Commissions on various matters including transport. Papers relating specifically to Ireland include those of the Vice-Regal Commission on Irish railways, 1906–10, and several other commisions at various dates.

RAIL 1124 Reports of Committees, n.d. These reports of and to Select and Departmental Committees consist almost entirely of printed Parliamentary Papers, including a certain amount of Irish material among them.

NOTE: In addition to the classes mentioned above, it will be worth searching through other general *RAIL* classes as well as those of English, Scottish and Welsh companies (e.g. *RAIL 1025*, labour and staff matters, 1912–56) for material on Ireland, on Irish individuals employed by non-Irish companies, etc.

RECO: Ministry of Reconstruction records

RECO 1 Records of the Ministry, 1915–20. They include those of the two reconstruction committees of the Cabinet which preceded it and of various committees and sub-committees appointed by them and by other departments. The Ministry of Reconstruction during the First World War laid the foundations for the major reorganisation of government into new departments (e.g. the Ministry of Health) which followed the war. Its records cover a very wide range of subjects and are often of special interest for the light they shed on new thinking about social administration in this period of upheaval and rapid change. References to Ireland are scattered throughout the class. For example, *RECO 1/936* deals with a coal boring scheme in Loch Neagh, Northern Ireland, in 1917–18 (with map); *RECO 1/939–63* contain replies to circular letters to county councils concerning rural development in the UK in 1918, with replies from various parts of Ireland; *RECO 1/524, 529, 602* and *606* deal with housing in Ireland; and *RECO 1/780, 785–6* relate to the Irish Reconstruction Association and formation of the Irish Department of Reconstruction and Development.

RG: Records of the General Register Office and Office of Population Censuses and Surveys.

(NOTE: Classes *RG 4–19, 27,* and *30–7* are kept at the PRO, Chancery Lane and Portugal Street. The remainder are kept at Kew)
The records in this group are most heavily used for local history and genealogical studies. Above all, the 19th-century censuses of population which become open to public inspection when they are 100 years old provide a rich source for genealogical research. Those for 1861, 1871 and 1881 are respectively in *RG 9–11*. Like the 1851 census in *HO 107* (see above), they give the county and parish of birth of every person born in England, but normally only the entry 'Ireland' appears beside the names of people of Irish birth, although sometimes the counties of birth are also given. All of these classes are normally consulted on microfilm (in order to protect the original from damage caused by excessive handling) in a special reading room run by the PRO in the Land Registry building, Portugal Street, London WC 2, a stone's throw away from the Chancery Lane Branch of the Office. See also *HO 107*, above. The genealogical uses of *RG* records are more fully described in a PRO leaflet (which includes a brief section on Irish genealogy) and PRO handbook no. 19, *Tracing your Ancestors in the Public Record Office*

(London, HMSO, 1981). Correspondence and papers relating to census returns, 1894–1938, are in *RG 19* including some files on Ireland. In addition to this and other classes of numerical censuses, the *RG* group contains records of social surveys undertaken by government for various purposes at different times.

RG 26 Correspondence and Papers relating to Population and Medical Statistics, 1910–54. The class includes correspondence with the Registrar-General of Northern Ireland.

RG 28 National Registration, Correspondence and Papers, 1915–24. The class relates to the administration of the National Registration Act, 1915, which provided for a register of all men and women between the ages of 15 and 65 who were not in the armed forces. The papers in this class include those of the Hayes Fisher committee on national registration. *RG 28/2* is a file on an estimate of the possible Irish contribution to the armed forces, 1915–19, and some general files will almost certainly contain references to Ireland.

SO: Signet Office Records

The Signet Office's primary business was to prepare King's Bills for royal grants, for example in cases of commissions, charters, creations of nobility and patents. A secondary function was to enter all letters despatched under the royal sign manual from the government to the Lord Lieutenant of Ireland. The Signet Office was abolished in 1851 under Stat. 14 & 15 Vict, c. 82, and its surviving duties passed to the Home Office. Irish affairs figure prominently among its records, which are listed in detail up to 1837 in PRO *Lists and Indexes*, no. XLIII (London, HMSO, 1914, available in the Kraus Reprint series).

SO 1 Irish Letter Books, 1627–1876. These have been calendared for the period up to 1670 in the *Calendar of State Papers, Ireland* (London, HMSO, 1900–11, available in the Kraus Reprints series) and for 1670–1704 in the *Calendar of State Papers, Domestic* (London, HMSO, 1895–1925, also available in the Kraus Reprints series). From 1776 onwards the entries in these letter books are mostly duplicated in the Home Office's Irish series of King's letter books, *HO 101*, except that letters on financial matters (e.g. pension, pay of regiments in Ireland, etc.) which do appear in the Signet Office series, are not entered in *HO 101*. This class is indexed in *SO 2*.

SO 2 Irish Letter Books: Indexes, 1643–1875. These indexes relate to *SO 1*.

SO 5 Miscellaneous Records, 1660–1875. They include fee books which for the period 1852–71 relate to fees on Irish instruments only, and entry books to Irish letters, 1800–6.

SP: Records of the Secretaries of State and State Paper Office

(NOTE: Kept at the PRO, Chancery Lane)
The main business of the state gradually came to be exercised during the

reign of Henry VIII by the King's Principal Secretary, and by the end of the same reign there were two principal secretaries. During the 17th century their business was divided according to the areas of foreign affairs that each one dealt with, so that the secretaries' office was divided into a Southern and a Northern Department. The existence of a State Paper Office and Keeper of the State Papers dates back to the early 17th century. During the 18th century, the system became progressively more unwieldy with the growth of government business, and in 1782 a complete overhaul of central administration resulted in the division of the old offices of Secretaries of State and their replacement by the more specialist Home Department and Foreign Office. The series of State Papers therefore reflect the main business of central government for the period roughly extending from the early years of Henry VIII's reign to 1782. With the exception of the early Tudor State Papers, they are divided into two main series, domestic and foreign. State Papers, Domestic, are divided into classes mainly chronologically by reign. State Papers, Foreign, are divided mainly according to the countries that they deal with. A multi-volume *Calendar of State Papers, Domestic* has been published by the HMSO for the period up to 1704 and is available in the Kraus series. The *Calendar of State Papers, Foreign* does not extend beyond the reign of Elizabeth I. There is also a *Calendar of State Papers, Colonial* which is drawn mainly from papers now in *CO* classes and covers the period 1574–1738. Irish material will be found throughout the State Papers, but especially for the period after 1700 with which this guide is concerned, in the following classes:

SP 63 State Papers, Ireland, Elizabeth I to George III, 1558–1782.

SP 65 State Papers, Ireland, Folios, 1536–1707.

SP 67 State Papers, Ireland, Miscellanea, 1681–1783. Indexed except for vol. 21 (1746–60).

NOTE: The Public Record Office of Northern Ireland, in Belfast, has transcripts of the State Papers, Ireland, from 1715 to 1767, made in London by the Deputy Keeper of the Public Records of Northern Ireland at various dates from 1928.

STAT: Records of HM Stationery Office
Records relating to government printing in *STAT* classes go back to 1785, and all *STAT* classes will be found to include a scattering of Irish business, particularly for the period before 1920. The main classes are arranged as follows:

STAT 1 In-Letters, 1798–1866. Most of these are from the Treasury.

STAT 2 Registers of In-Letters, from 1855. These relate to files in *STAT 1, 12* and *14*.

STAT 3 Out-letters, from 1785. Entry books and copies of letters to the

Treasury, 1785–1920; to Ireland and Scotland, 1832–1918; War Office, 1860–1909; Board of Works, 1860–5; and to miscellaneous recipients from 1802. The first volume for each year generally contains an index to all volumes for that year.

STAT 4 Copyright Out-Letters, from 1888. Copies of out-letters relating to copyright, generally indexed in the first volume for each year. Volumes for 1921–36 are missing.

STAT 6 Controller's Private Letter Books, from 1846. Entry books and copies of official and semi-official out-letters.

STAT 7 Miscellanea, from 1792.

STAT 12 Files of Correspondence, Series, I, from 1858.

STAT 13 Establishment and Accounting Records, from 1786.

STAT 14 Files of Correspondence, Series II, from 1871.

T: Records of the Treasury
The Treasury is responsible for the control and management of the entire public revenue and its expenditure. The character and extent of this control have varied from time to time, developing with the extension of parliamentary control over finance. It is primarily a policy department, and is responsible to Parliament for the imposition and regulation of taxation and for monetary policy. It is also the primary instrument for controlling the expenditure by departments of money voted by Parliament, and associated with this are its duties as the controlling and co-ordinating department for all matters connected with the management, pay and conditions of service of the Civil Service. The Treasury is a prerogative department and many of its powers are not derived from statute. It has therefore always been deeply involved in Irish affairs at all levels and in every aspect of government business, ranging from police matters to agricultural policy and the administration of the Irish Land Acts, though its precise relationship with different departments of the Irish administration varied greatly in detail and at different times. The main classes in which material relevant to Irish history will be found are as follows:

T 1 Treasury Board Papers, 1557–1920. Correspondence together with reports and draft minutes. These papers, along with the contents of several other *T* classes, are calendared up to 1745 in the *Calendar of Treasury Papers* (1557–1728), *Calendar of Treasury Books* (1660–1718) and *Calendar of Treasury Books and Papers* (1729–45) (London, HMSO, 1868–1962, mostly available in the Kraus Reprint series). They relate to virtually the whole range of government business, since the Treasury's supervision of finance caused it to be involved at some stage in the work of all other government departments. Out-letters from the Treasury were entered in separate series of volumes from a relatively early stage, but this main series of in-letters remained virtually undivided until the complete overhaul of the registration system that took place in 1920. This massive collection of 12,626 volumes, bundles and boxes is arranged chronologically and in order of file numbers for each year. The registers which are essential finding aids to it are in *T 2–3*, with some earlier registers in *T 4* and from 1852 indexes in *T 108*. See also *T 14*, below.

T 2 Registers of Papers, 1777–1920. These give the dates and subject-matter of the files in *T 1*. They have to be used in conjunction with the skeleton registers in *T 3*, which record transfers of file numbers.

T 3 Skeleton Registers, 1783–1920.

T 4 Reference Books, 1680–1819. Entries of petitions to the Treasury, plus some early registers of papers in *T 1* and a series of indexes to letters from abroad.

T 11 Out-Letters, Customs, 1667–1922. They include excise matters, 1664–71, 1801–49 and 1909–22.

T 14 Out-Letters, Ireland, 1669–1924. Letters on Irish matters and to Irish departments, to the Treasury Remembrancer in Ireland and to Irish local authorities and individuals. For the period June 1920–October 1922, see *T 158* and *192*.

T 28 Various Out-Letters, 1763–1885. These include five volumes of letters on public works in Ireland, 1831–1956.

T 37 Accounts, Ireland, 1692–1865. A miscellaneous class including accounts of weekly income and expenditure, 1822–45, and Consolidated Fund schedules, 1843–59.

T 38 Departmental Accounts, 1558–1937. Amongst the quantity of administrative sub-headings under which these papers are arranged, those that seem likely to include Irish material or references to Irish individuals are: convict hulks, 1802–51, quarterly lists of crews and convicts, sickness returns, etc. (see also *HO* classes); customs accounts of receipts and payments, reign of Elizabeth I to 1835; and secret service cash and receipt books, 1689–1710.

T 48 Lowndes Papers, reign of Charles I to 1886. Books and papers of William Lowndes, Secretary of the Treasury, 1695–1724, including various papers on Ireland.

T 64 Various Papers, 1547–1905. Amongst the considerable proportion of this class relating to Ireland, the subject-matter includes: shipping estimates (reign of James I to 1848); Irish pensions and establishment (various dates); imports and exports; potato crop returns, 1848; unemployment returns, 1848; and papers of Sir Charles Trevelyan (Assistant Secretary to the Treasury, 1840–59) mainly relating to administration and famine relief in Ireland in 1846–9. The class list of *T 64*, kept in the reference room of the

PRO, Kew, includes a fairly detailed description of the Trevelyan papers, which comprise *T 64/362A–370C*

T 80 War Compensation Papers, 1915–28. They include awards and minutes of evidence of the Irish Deportees (Compensation) Tribunal.

T 91 Irish Reproductive Loan Fund, 1822–74. Mostly arranged by local associations and county committees and trusts, but also including a number of general directors' papers on policy, regulations, particular loans, etc.

T 103 Papers relating to Irish Corporations, 1842–1903. Files of correspondence, etc. on loans raised by Irish corporations.

T 143 Out-Letters, Irish Treasury Remembrancer, 1911–17.

T 158 Out-Letters Treasury (Ireland), 1920–2. Out-letter books of the Treasury Office in Dublin containing letters to Irish departments and local authorities and to the Treasury in London. For earlier correspondence see *T 14*.

T 160–3 Finance, Supply, Establishment and General Files, from 1887. The four series overlap with the papers in *T 1* but between them take over the functions of *T 1* from 1920. They are arranged under subject headings which include no separate heading for Ireland, but they are well worth searching nevertheless for papers relating to various aspects of administration in Ireland. To take two examples, *T 162/621/E8341* is a file entitled 'Treasury Work relating to Ireland', in the establishment series, and *T 163*, general series, includes a large quantity of material relating to administrative changes in 1920–2.

T 168 Hamilton Papers, 1847–1913. Papers of George Alexander Hamilton (1802–71), a high-ranking Treasury official from the 1850s and finally Assistant, then Permanent Secretary to the Treasury, 1859–70; and of Sir Edward Hamilton (1848–1908) who was also a high-ranking Treasury official for many years and joint Permanent Secretary, 1902–7. These include various papers relating to Ireland, e.g. files dated 1894–6 on financial relations between England and Ireland.

T 172 Chancellor of the Exchequer's Office, Miscellaneous Papers, from 1792. They contain a number of papers on various aspects of Irish affairs, e.g. a report of the Commissariat General dated 1843, on frauds committed by the accountant in the Office of Public Works, Ireland (*T 172/930*); papers on the appointment of a commissioner to the Irish Land Valuation Office, 1911–12 (*T 172/53*); various Irish deputations; papers on the Government of Ireland Bill, 1919–20 (*TY 172/1090*); papers on Irish land purchase in 1922 (*T 172/1293*), etc.

T 175 Private Office Papers and Private Collections: Hopkins Papers, 1914–42. They include *T 175/24* on the proposed Irish Free State loan in 1928.

T 176 Private Office Papers and Private Collections: Niemeyer Papers, 1915–30. Two pieces in this class relate to finances in the Irish Free State, in 1923 and 1925 respectively.

T 186 Hardman Lever Papers, 1919–22. Sir Hardman Lever was appointed in 1919 to act as the Treasury's representative in the newly formed Ministry of Transport and to supervise all financial transactions relating to roads, railways and canals. These papers relate to his activities in that post, August 1919–October 1921, and include a quantity of material on transport (mainly but not only railways) in Ireland.

T 188 Leith-Ross Papers, 1898–1968. Official, semi-official and some private papers of Sir Frederick Leith-Ross (1887–1968). Leith-Ross's long and distinguished career in public service included the post of private secretary to the Prime Minister, H.H. Asquith, 1911–13, and his papers from this period include one piece relating to Irish home rule, 1898–1913. A small scattering of references to Ireland will also be found in other papers in the class.

T 192 Ireland: Files, 1920–2. The files in this class are those of A. R. Waterfield, who was Treasury Remembrancer in Ireland during the period when the Treasury exercised control of all fresh expenditure in Ireland, conducting all Irish business in Dublin. These files deal mainly with pensions and other financial matters and with administrative matters under the National School Teachers (Ireland) Act, 1879. There is a related file on 'Treasury work relating to Ireland' in *T 162/621/E8241*.

T 201 Certificate, Memorandum and Account Books, These volumes, of various dates from 1793 to 1893, were compiled in the Revenue department and its successor, within the Treasury, and contain entries of minutes, accounts and other notes on subjects including the expenses of civil government in Ireland.

T 208 Financial Enquiries Branch (Hawtrey) Papers, 1859–1940. These papers date mainly from the period of office of (Sir) Ralph Hawtrey, director of the branch from 1919 to 1946. They include files on a wide range of general financial matters of interest to the Treasury, and a few relate to Irish affairs, e.g. to financial provisions under the Government of Ireland Bill.

T 221 Law and Order Division Files, from 1880. Most of these files date from after 1948, when the Treasury adopted a decentralised registry system. They include various papers on the costs of administering law and order (including elections) in Northern Ireland.

T 229 Central Economic Planning Section Files, from 1939. Most of these files date from 1947 or later, when the Treasury took over responsibility for the Central Economic Planning Staff. *T 299/93* deals with Northern Ireland, 'help in export drive and economic difficulties, 1947'. Other general files bear on the United Kingdom as a whole, including Northern Ireland.

T 233 Home Finance Division Files, from 1948. The subjects covered by this division of the Treasury include the Irish Sailors and Soldiers Land Trust and financial arrangements in Northern Ireland.

T 236 Overseas Finance Division Files, from 1920. A small proportion of these files relating to many different aspects of overseas financial policy and negotiations directly concerns financial and economic relations with the Irish Republic after 1945.

T 237 Overseas Finance (Marshall Aid). The class contains three pieces (*T 237/94–6*) dealing with the administration of the European Reconstruction Programme (Marshall Aid) in the Irish Republic, 1948–52.

T 239 Register of Daily Receipts, from 1855. These registers record daily receipts in the Exchequer account at the Banks of England and Ireland. Those for the years 1911–32 have not survived.

T 241 Bank of England Papers, 1808–1946. These include some references to dealings with the Bank of Ireland.

T 250 Private Office Papers: Welby Papers, 1818–1910. These consist mainly of printed material used by Sir Reginald (later Lord) Welby both before and after his appointment as Permanent Secretary to the Treasury, 1885–94. They also include some papers of his predecessor, Lord Lingen. One volume contains Irish Church Commission reports, etc., 1854–84 and three volumes deal with Irish land, 1854–94, including papers of the Irish Land Commission.

T 257 Ledgers and Journals, 1854–1915. These are the double-entry book-keeping records of all transactions day by day on the accounts of HM Exchequer at the Banks of England and Ireland.

TS: Records of the Treasury Solicitor and HM Procurator General
(NOTE: Kept at the PRO, Chancery Lane)
The duties of the Treasury Solicitor, an office which dates back to 1655 or even earlier, consisted primarily until 1842 of advising the King's Counsel on revenue cases. After 1842 he acted as legal adviser to an increasing number of government departments, between 1884 and 1908 he functioned as Director of Public Prosecutions in addition to his other duties and since 1876 the office has been held in conjunction with that of HM Procurator General, whose formerly many and various functions were reduced by that time mainly to intervention in matrimonial causes and to the conduct of prize proceedings in the UK in time of war. Various statutory changes during the centuries that the Office of Treasury Solicitor has existed (the introduction of new procedure for treason trials in the 19th century, for example) have resulted in the accrual of papers on a very wide variety of subjects in *TS* classes, and they are well worth searching closely for Irish material. Note especially the following:

TS 11 Papers, 1584–1856. These are papers in the various legal proceedings dealt with by the Treasury Solicitor and HM Procurator General. They relate to state trials, the preservation of the public peace, escheats and administrations cases, and much else. Irish material will be found scattered throughout.

TS 18 General Series Papers, from 1517. This class consists of papers of the 18th to 20th centuries, some of which are copies of earlier documents. It deals with cases on which the Treasury Solicitor's legal advice or service were sought, and includes papers on Irish troubles at various dates.

TS 24 Sedition Cases, Miscellaneous Papers, 1732–1901. A mixture of official correspondence and other material relating to prosecutions for seditious libel. Most of the papers reflect the activities of various societies working for freedom of speech and parliamentary reform in the 1790s and the second decade of the 19th century. They include some Irish pamphlets.

TS 27 Registered Files, Treasury and Miscellaneous Series, from 1843. They include various opinions on cases involving Ireland.

TS 31 Statutory Publications Office Papers, 1882–1941. These files relating mainly to editorial matters connected with the publications by the Treasury Solicitor include one (*TS 31/9*) on Irish matters, 1898–1922.

UGC: Records of the University Grants Committee.
The University Grants Committee has been in existence since 1919, when it was set up 'to inquire into the financial needs of university education in the United Kingdom and to advise the government as to the applications of any grants made by Parliament towards meeting them'. The following class is of particular interest for Irish historians:

UGC 5 Miscellanea, 1911–42. Pieces 9–12 deal with universities and colleges in Ireland between 1918 and 1942.

WO: Records of the War Office, Board of Ordnance and Army Departments.
This extensive group of records and its administrative background are described in some detail in the *Guide to the Contents of the Public Record Office*, vol. II, and in the current *Guide*, parts I and II. An *Alphabetical Guide to War Office and Other Military Records Preserved in the Public Record Office* is published as PRO *Lists and Indexes*, vol. LIII (London, HMSO, 1931, available in the Kraus reprint series). Any number of *WO* classes will be worth searching for the purposes of the Irish genealogist or biographer, for the records of Irish regiments, and individual Irish soldiers and officers. The activities of the War Office and Army in Ireland from the late 16th century onwards are reflected also in many different classes. It must be emphasised that no attempt has been made here to identify all the potential sources of Irish material in *WO* records. The following, however, are particularly well worth mentioning:

WO 1 In-Letters, 1732–1868. This large class is arranged under the various military stations or public departments from which the letters were sent, or by subject-matter or alphabetically by the name of the writer. There are various sources of Irish material in the class, among them some papers of the Prince de Bouillon (for whom see above, under *FO 95*). These form *WO 1/921–26* covering the period 1794–1816, and are listed in detail with a very full introduction in the typescript list of *WO 1*, available on the reference room shelves at the PRO, Kew. Their subject-matter includes the political situation in Ireland and French arms supplies for Ireland.

WO 8 Ireland Out-Letters, 1710–1823. Entry books of the Muster Master General of Ireland, of royal warrants and letters and warrants of the Lords Justices General and the Governors General of Ireland relating to the military establishment there.

WO 10 Artillery Muster Books and Pay Lists, 1708–1878. These include particulars of Irish regiments and of regiments serving in Ireland. Continued in *WO 16*.

WO 12 General Muster Books and Pay Lists, 1732–1838. They include Irish regiments and depots. Continued in *WO 16*.

WO 13 Militia and Volunteers Muster Books and Pay Lists, 1780–1878. The class includes the Irish militia and yeomanry, arranged under counties.

WO 16 New Series Muster Book and Paylists, 1877–98. A continuation of *WO 10* and *12*.

WO 2504 Various Registers, 1660–1928. They include entries on the defence of Ireland, 1801–86.

WO 30 Miscellanea, 1684–1933. The class includes reports, papers, itineraries, etc. relating to the defence of Great Britain and Ireland, 1756–1873; and papers on the erection of Irish barracks, 1849.

WO 31 Commander-In-Chief Memoranda Papers, 1793–1870. These consist of memoranda of appointments, promotions and resignations, filed with original applications, covering letters from commanding officers, army agents, etc. The class includes a distinct series of schedules from Ireland, 1801–59.

WO 32 Registered Papers, General Series, 1855–1971. Documents selected for permanent preservation from the main series of registered files of the War Office, and relating to all aspects of War Office business. They are arranged under subject codes under which two examples of Irish sub-headings are: 'Employment of military forces, Irish Rebellion (1916–20), code 53G'; and 'Overseas, Ireland, code 0/AD'. Subject indexes to these papers are in *WO 139*.

WO 33 Reports and Miscellaneous Papers, from 1853. This collection of printed reports, memoranda, etc. is separate from other series because the papers it contains were originally subject to a special security classification and were specially printed and given a limited circulation. They include a scattering of papers relevant to Ireland, e.g. *WO 33/882*, instructions for the Commander-in-Chief, Ireland, in 1918.

WO 35 Ireland, 1775–1923. Records relating to the establishment and administration of the army in Ireland, etc., plus papers dealing with the 'troubles' of 1914–22. These include: records of the Curragh incident and Easter rising of 1916; raid and search reports; war diaries; proceedings of military and civil courts; and files containing biographical details of men and women prominent in the Irish nationalist movements.

WO 44 Ordnance Office In-Letters, 1682–1873. The bulk of the class relates to the first half of the 19th century. It includes a section dealing specifically with barracks, army supplies and related matters in Ireland. Registers to the class are in *WO 45*.

WO 47 Ordnance Office Minutes, 1644–1856. These include copies of minutes of the proceedings of the Office of Ordnance, Dublin, 1826–31, which were transmitted to the Board of Ordnance. Other sub-sections of this class also include references to Ireland, e.g. papers relating to barrack masters (Ireland) 1834–8, and the main series of minutes of proceedings of the Board of Ordnance, which constitute the bulk of this class, are worth searching for material of Irish relevance. See also Ordnance Office records in *WO 49*, and *WO 54–5*, below.

WO 49 Ordnance Office Various Accounts, 1592–1858. The subject matter of these accounts includes Irish expenditure.

WO 54 Ordnance Office Registers, 1594–1871. Entry books and registers of the Ordnance Office including some lists of the establishment of the Irish Ordnance Office establishment.

WO 55 Ordnance Office Miscellanea, 1568–1923. The class includes a series of artillery letters and letter books relating to Ireland, 1825–39. Other sub-sections of the class also contain occasional Irish papers.

WO 63 Commissariat Department, Ireland, 1797–1852. The class consists of letter books, cash accounts, journals, and ledgers of the Commissariat headquarters in Dublin and of Commissariat centres during the Irish famine.

WO 68 Militia Records, 1759–1925. Records of militia regiments in Great Britain and Ireland. These are useful for geneaological and biographical purposes and also include regimental histories and statistical particulars.

WO 71 Judge Advocate General's Office, Courts Martial Proceedings, from 1668. These include some special returns from Ireland between 1800 and 1820.

WO 78 Maps and Plans, from 1627. Compiled or collected by the Ordnance Survey, Ordnance Office, topographical branches of the War Office, the Commander-in-Chief and the Directorate of Fortifications and Works, they relate to the United Kingdom and overseas. The class includes a section on Ireland.

WO 79 Various Private Collections, 1709–1937. The class includes records of the Connaught Rangers and the Galway and Roscommon Militias, 1793–1919.

WO 80 Murray Papers, 1804–59. Correspondence and memoranda of Sir George Murray who was Commander-in-Chief in Ireland, 1825–8. The class includes a private letter book relating to military affairs in Ireland, 1825–7.

WO 96 Militia Attestation Documents, 1806–1915. These forms were filled in at the time of recruitment and usually annotated to the date of discharge form a record of each individual's service. They are arranged by counties, including Irish counties.

WO 97 Royal Hospital, Chelsea, Soldiers' Documents, 1760–1900. This is the main series of service documents of soldiers who became in- or out-pensioners of the Royal Hospital Chelsea. The documents are arranged under the names of regiment, including Irish ones.

WO 118 Royal Hospital, Kilmainham, Admission Books, 1704–1922. Registers of out-pensioners of the army and militia from the Royal Hospital, Kilmainham, including dates of admission and sometimes of death. The class includes indexes to entry books prior to November 1822 and to the documents in *WO 119*.

WO 119 Royal Hospital, Kilmainham, Discharge Documents of Pensioners, to 1822. These are certificates of service of pensioners of the hospital and are indexed in *WO 118*. Some other certificates of the hospital are in *WO 900*.

WO 132 Buller Papers, 1872–1901. Official and semi-official correspondence, reports, etc. of Sir Redvers Buller while he served in various capacities, including those of Special Commissioner of Police in Ireland and then Deputy Secretary for Ireland, 1886–7. One piece, containing letters from W.H. Smith, Secretary of State for War, 1886, is closed for 100 years (i.e. until 1987).

WO 137 Private Office Papers: Derby Papers, 1921–3. They were accumulated in the private office of the Secretary of State for War when the post was filled by Edward, seventeeth Earl of Derby. They include a few papers on Ireland.

WO 139 Subject Indexes, 1826–1901. These subject registers provide a digest of the chief correspondence of the War Office, mainly referring to the registered papers in *WO 32*, before the extensive weeding of that class.

WO 199 War of 1939–45. Military Headquarters Papers, Home Forces, 1914–56. These policy, planning and administrative files are arranged by subject and in command order, and include papers on the headquarters, Northern Ireland district.

WO 900 Specimens of Classes of Documents Destroyed. These include four pensioners' certificates from the Royal Hospital, Kilmainham, 1798–1817 (see above, *WO 118–19*).

WORK: *Records of the Office of Works, Ministry of Public Buildings and Work and other works departments.*
Records in the *WORK* group relate to public buildings and works from the 17th century onwards, and in many cases overlap with records in other groups, reflecting the various aspects of government buildings, etc. through the centuries. A scattering of Irish material will be found in several *WORK* classes, but note especially the following:

WORK 6 Miscellanea, from 1609. This class includes papers on public buildings, roads and other works in Ireland, 1835–85.

WORK 27 Files on Public Buildings in Northern Ireland, from 1921.

WORK 42 Maps and Plans of Public Buildings in Northern Ireland, 1920–9. All twenty-five drawings and plans in this class relate to the Parliament buildings.

CLASSES OF RECORDS RELATING ENTIRELY TO IRISH AFFAIRS.

ADM	148–50		PMG	48
AP	1–6		PRO	30/59, 89; 31/1
CO	697–9; 739; 761–2; 783–5; 903–6		RAIL	131; 162; 206; 327; 941
			SO	1–2
CUST	1		SP	63; 65; 67
DO	37; 99; 100; 130		T	14; 37; 91; 103; 158 192
HO	100–1; 121; 123; 161; 184; 219; 246; 248		WO	8; 35; 118–19
			WORK	27; 42
NDO	3			

INDEX

NOTE: References are to entries in the text and not to the Introduction. Where reference is made to a group of records without a class number (e.g. *CAB*, *FO*, *MAF*) this indicates either that the subject appears in the introductory remarks for the group or that it appears frequently within the group.

Abbot, Charles, 1st Baron Colchester (1757–1829) *PRO 30/9*
accounts *AMD 49*; *AO*; *MINT*; *T 37–8, 201, 257*; *WO 49, 63*
Acts of Parliament *RAIL 1062–4*
  see also particular Acts by name; parliamentary bills
Admiralty *ADM*; *AIR 1*; *MT 2, 19, 32*
agriculture *AP*; *MAF*; *PRO 30/64*; *PWLB*; *T*
air forces *AIR 8*
  see also Royal Air Force
Air Historical Branch *AIR*, *AIR 1, 5*
Air Ministry *AIR*
Aldworth family *PRO 30/50*
Allan, Maj.-Gen. Alexander (?–1881)
  papers on ecclesiastical history *PRO 30/2*
Anderson, Sir Robert (1841–1918) *HO 144*
Annan Committee
  see Committee on the Future of Broadcasting
appointments and honours *CUST 110*; *HO 45, 141*; *PREM 2, 5*; *T 172*; *WO 3*
apprenticeship books *IR 1, 17*
approved societies *ACT 2*; *NIA*
Ardagh, Maj.-Gen. Sir John (1840–1907) *PRO 30/40*
army departments *WO*
Art Union of Ireland *BT 1*
Asquith, Herbert, 1st Earl of Oxford and Asquith (1852–1925) *T 188*
Assistance Board *AST*
  see also National Assistance Board; Unemployment Assistance Board
Assize courts *ASSI*
Audit Office *AO*
  see also Exchequer and Audit Department; Irish Audit Office
Auditors of Land Revenue *LR*
Australia *CO*; *DO*; *HO*
Austria, *FO 95, 944*

Balfour, Arthur (1848–1930) *PRO 30/60*
Balfour, Gerald (1853–1945) *PRO 30/60*
Bank of England *T 239, 241, 257*
Bank of Ireland *LRRO 54*; *MINT 6, 9*; *T 239, 241, 257*
bankruptcy
  see Court of Bankruptcy
barracks, *OS 5*; *WO 30, 44, 47*
Barrett, Michael (?–1868) *HO 12*
Belfast
  Royal Courts of Justice *DSIR 4*
  war damage *IR 37*

Bentinck, William Cavendish, 3rd Duke of Portland (1738–1809) *PRO 30/58*
Beveridge, William, 1st Baron (1879–1963)
  national insurance plan *ACT 1*
Board of Customs *CUST*
Board of Customs and Excise *AST*; *CUST*
Board of Excise *CUST*; *IR 83*
Board of Inland Revenue *CUST 47*; *IR*
Board of Ordnance *WO*; *WO 47*
Board of Stamps *IR 1, 31, 43, 49–50, 72, 83*
Board of Stamps and Taxes *IR 31, 83–4*
Board of Taxes *IR*
Board of Trade *AST*; *BT*; *CRES 42*; *PRO 30/60*
  Commercial Department *BT 11–12, 35–36*
  Companies Registration Office *BT 31, 34, 41*
  Industries and Manufactures Department *BT 64*
  Labour Departments *LAB*
  Marine and Harbour Departments *CRES 42*; *MT*
  Patent Office *BT 42–53*; *900*
  Railway Department *MT 6–7, 11–13, 91*
  see also Ministry of Transport
Board of Works *STAT 3*; *WORK*
Bouillon, Prince de
  see d'Auvergne
British Rail *RAIL*
British Transport Commission *RAIL*
British Transport Historical Records *RAIL*
British War Pensions Advisory Committee *PIN 15*
broadcasting *HO 244–5*
Broderick, St John, 1st Earl of Midleton (1856–1942) *PRO 30/67*
Buckingham, 1st Marquis of, *see* Grenville, George Nugent-Temple-
building and loan societies *FS*
building research *DSIR 4*
Buller, Sir Redvers (1839–1908) *WO 132*
business undertakings *B*; *BT*; *PWLB*

Cabinet Office *CAB*
  conferences on Ireland *CAB 43*
  Dardanelles Committee *CAB 42*
  Irish Situation Committee *PRO 30/69*
  Reconstruction Secretariat *CAB 117*
  War Committee and Council *CAB 42*
  See also Committee of Imperial Defence
Cairns, 1st Earl
  see McCalmont, Hugh
Calonne, Comte de (1734–1802) *FO 95*; *PC 1*